Tim Pat Coogan, one of Ireland's most prominent journalists, is also well known as an historian, broadcaster and writer. He has appeared on television in most English-speaking countries and throughout Europe, and has written for a number of Irish, European and American publications, including the *Sunday Times* and the *New York Times*. He was appointed editor of the *Irish Press* in 1968. His first book, *Ireland Since the Rising* (1966), was the first history of that period. His definitive history, *The IRA*, which has been constantly revised and updated, followed in 1970, and *The Irish: A Personal View* was published in 1975. He has written biographies of Michael Collins and Eamon de Valera. His most recent books include *The Irish Civil War* (with George Morrison, 1998) and *The Irish Diaspora* (2001).

1916:
The Easter Rising

TIM PAT COOGAN

PHOENIX

A PHOENIX PAPERBACK

First published in Great Britain in 2001
by Cassell & Co.
This paperback edition published in 2005
by Phoenix,
an imprint of Orion Books Ltd,
Orion House, 5 Upper St Martin's Lane,
London WC2H 9EA

A CIP catalogue record for this book
is available from the British Library.

ISBN 0 75381 852 3

Printed and bound in Great Britain by
Clays Ltd, St Ives plc

www.orionbooks.co.uk

To Charles and Wilma Mooney,
friends to me and to Ireland.

Contents

A CAUTIONARY TALE FOR TODAY   1

THE 1916 EASTER RISING   5

AFTERMATH   171

SELECT BIBLIOGRAPHY   181

ENDNOTES   183

INDEX   189

A Cautionary Tale for Today

...either character or circumstance may be the basis of a
sunkrisis *(comparison); similar events affecting dissimilar*
persons and similar persons reacting to contrasting events
alike provide a suitable field for the exercise. It is basically a
rhetorical procedure: but it is rescued from purely rhetorical
ingenuity by its value as a way of concentrating and directing
the moral reflections which are the primary purpose of
biography.

D. A. Russell, PLUTARCH *(London, 1973)*

The 1916 Rising was both profoundly important and profoundly unnecessary. Widely and rightly hailed as a high
water mark of the Green or Catholic and Nationalist tradition, it was in fact triggered off by the Orange and Protestant
tradition and its British allies. Redmond Howard, a politically aware witness to the Rising and a critic of the rebels,
wrote in its aftermath: 'There never was, I believe, an Irish
crime – if crime it can be called – which had not its roots in an
English folly.' His words are still relevant. The genesis of 1916
has an uncanny resemblance to contemporary Irish events in
certain significant regards. For although one ushered in a
period of violent change, the other (hopefully) of peaceful
alteration, nevertheless if one changes the word 'biography'
to 'history' in the foregoing quote, one finds that Russell's
thesis of *sunkrisis* becomes disturbingly apposite when
applied to the 1916 Rising and to what may validly be termed

Easter Two, the Good Friday Agreement of 1998. In both cases, a majority of political opinion in Ireland, England and amongst the Irish diaspora was and is in favour of a certain process being given legislative effect. In what might be termed Easter One, that of 1916, an overwhelming majority in favour of Home Rule was registered some four years before the Rising broke out, at the time when the third Home Rule Bill was introduced in 1912.

In the case of the contemporary Peace Process, there was equally overwhelming support for the ceasefire declared by the Provisional IRA on 31 August, 1994, four years before Easter Two, when the Good Friday Agreement was finally signed. Both processes were destined to be seriously impeded by the Ulster Unionists and their English Conservative allies in politics and the army. These are nothing like as potent now as they were in 1916. But they are not without a malign efficacy nonetheless. Ominously too, just as in 1916 a small segment of the physical force school of Irish Nationalism, like their counterparts in the Volunteers of 1916, have declared no confidence in the constitutional process and have placed their faith in violent means to achieve their ends. This decision has resulted in a series of bombing attacks ranging from the Omagh atrocity in Ireland to an explosion at BBC Centre in London. Whether the group responsible, the so-called Real IRA, has the remotest possibility of achieving anything of the effect of the 1916 men is debatable to say the least.

What the four years of contemporary delay and their stagnant aftermath of two further years of squandered opportunity will ultimately lead to, nobody knows. But in grappling with the challenges posed by the Real IRA and the recalcitrant Orangemen, it is at least instructive and at worst alarming to examine what four years of delay and extra parliamentary defiance led to in 1916, a date that still holds all the sacrificial significance of High Mass for Irish Republicans. Ultimately, modern Ireland and its two states were created. But these were achieved at the cost of the vicious Black and Tan war which broke out after the Rising, the even more vicious Irish Civil War which followed the ending of Anglo-Irish hostilities and the partition of Ireland. This last was responsible for a murderous pogrom and population displacement of Catholics. There followed the creation of an apartheid system of government – the institutionalisation of discrimination and gerrymandering as methods of preventing a rise in the Catholic vote in the 1920s. The results were a divided community, various intermittent outbreaks of violence and the thirty continuous years of 'the Troubles', which the Good Friday Agreement was intended to put an end to for ever.

When looked at against the contemporary background of the faltering Peace Process, the 1916 Rising is transformed from being an historical event into a cautionary tale for today. To tell the tale of Easter Week by merely reciting the events which occurred that fateful April would be analogous to attempting to describe the development of the American West solely by reference to events such as the shoot-out at the OK Corral. Granted that the Rising was a seminal event in Irish history, and that out of it modern Ireland emerged, and as the poet said, all was changed, changed utterly. But it is what has not changed that matters, namely the resistance of a sizeable section of Protestant opinion in north-eastern Ireland to the Peace Process, and the continuing involvement of the Conservative Party and sections of the British security forces in that resistance. Set in that context, 1916 becomes no faraway historical event but a cautionary tale. While I hope to give the average intelligent reader a good general grasp of what happened in 1916, I have also attempted to bring home the lesson that the message of 1916 is as vitally important today as it was then. The message is that those who do not learn from history really can be doomed to relive it...

The 1916 Easter Rising

THE ROSE TREE

But where can we draw water,
Said Pearse to Connolly,
When all the wells are parched away?
O plain as plain can be
There's nothing but our own red blood
Can make a right Rose Tree.

The play scheduled for the Abbey Theatre that night was Yeats's *Cathleen Ni Houlihan*.[1] In it, Cathleen Ni Houlihan (Ireland) is an old woman who appears in a house where a wedding has been prepared on the eve of the 1798 Rebellion. She says that she is buoyed up by 'the hope of getting my beautiful fields back again; the hope of putting the strangers out of my house'. By the end of the play, she has been transformed into a young girl with 'the walk of a queen', and the prospective bridegroom has left to join the Rebels, of whom the old woman says:

They shall be speaking forever,
The people shall hear them forever.

It was an uncannily appropriate production, in more ways than one. The stage drama had to be postponed because the street theatre outside took over. Cathleen Ni Houlihan no longer graces the Abbey boards, but in a real sense the old lady's wishes are still echoed in some quarters in Ireland

and at the time of writing, the play goes on.

The reason it does so is contained in the same pithy sentence which led to the 1916 Rising: 'Ulster will fight and Ulster will be right'. It is also the reason why six of Ireland's north-eastern counties are still ruled from London and why in 1998 three sovereign governments, those of the Republic of Ireland, the United Kingdom and America, involved themselves with Irish political parties in negotiating the Good Friday Agreement which it was vainly hoped would settle the argument over the 'beautiful fields'.

The significance of that sentence lies not merely in its wording, but in its context and its source. The context was the debate in late nineteenth-century England and Ireland on the issue of introducing Home Rule to Ireland. The source was a senior British Conservative, Lord Randolph Churchill, who addressed his audience in an artfully duplicitous manner which became the *leit motif* of the Conservatives' utilisation of the Irish question for domestic political gain. Churchill told his audience of Belfast Unionists that he was with them, as was his ancestor, the Duke of Marlborough, who had been a general of William of Orange, the Orangemen's icon; he neglected to remind them that the Duke had also been a general of William's enemy, the Catholic James II whom William defeated at the Battle of the Boyne in 1690. More importantly, along with telling his hearers that they would be right to fight, he gave Ulster Unionists a pledge that if Home Rule was attempted,[2] 'there will not be wanting to you those of position and influence in England who are willing to cast in their lot with you, whatever it may be, and who will share your fortune and your fate'.

The meeting held on 22 February, 1886 in the Ulster Hall had been advertised in the *Belfast News Letter* as a 'conservative demonstration – a monster meeting of Conservatives and Orangemen'. Churchill's presence and the commitments he made thus gave a benison to a remarkable feature of the Orange philosophy – its ability to preach 'loyalty', constitutionalism and religious liberty while at the same time either threatening or practising treason, violence, the arousal of sectarian hatred and the denial of human rights. Churchill returned to London, leaving in his wake violent Orange demonstrations and burning Catholic homes. In the long history of Protestant-Catholic animosities 1886 still stands out as a particularly bad year for sectarian violence. Not all the violence may fairly be laid at Churchill's door; rioting between Protestants and Catholics had been a feature of Belfast life since as far back as 1813, but his contribution and the use made of the Home Rule issue, both by the Conservatives in London and the Unionist leadership in Northern Ireland, certainly helped to inflame the situation.

A second reading of the Home Rule Bill triggered off rioting in Belfast. Protestant shipwrights drove Catholics from their dockland employment, forcing some into the waters of the Lagan, drowning one young man. Attack begat counterattack, and in a summer of discontent, some 32 people were killed, 371 injured and some £90,000 worth of property destroyed.

In helping Belfast to arrive at that level of dementia Churchill acted quite deliberately. Six days before making his Belfast speech, he wrote to a friend saying that he had 'decided some time ago that if the GOM went for Home

Rule, the Orange Card would be the one to play. Please God it may turn out the Ace of Trumps, and not the two'. Churchill's prayers were answered. Gladstone, the GOM (Grand Old Man), did introduce a Home Rule Bill for Ireland and the Orange Card turned up trumps. A number of Liberal Unionists sided with the Conservatives and the Bill, which incidentally only provided for a very limited form of self-government within the British Empire, went down. Nevertheless, in the subsequent general election, Ireland returned eighty-six Home Rule members against seventeen Unionists. This Irish percentage continued to be recorded in general elections for more than thirty years, but to no avail. In fact, the percentage would remain much the same a century later for the vote on the Good Friday Agreement of 1998 which also contained a measure of Home Rule for part of Northern Ireland. The votes that counted were not those cast in Ireland but in the parliamentary balance at Westminster.

Tory and Unionist opinion here was correctly summed up by a candidate in the general election of 1887 brought on by the Home Rule controversy. George Joachim Goschen (later First Viscount), a Liberal Unionist standing in Liverpool, declared:[3] 'We cannot allow the discontent of some three million inhabitants of the United Kingdom to reduce more than thirty million to impotence'. Lord Salisbury joined in the fray. He was a descendant of Lord Burleigh, one of the original lords of the Irish Plantation, and a prime minister of England. In an address to the Primrose League at Covent Garden he stated that Parliament had the right to govern Ulster but it had no right to sell its people into slavery. He said he did not believe in the unrestricted power of Parliament any more than he did in the unrestricted power of kings. He reminded his audience that James II had stepped outside the limits of the constitution and had been summarily dealt with by 'the people of Ulster'. He pointedly told his audience that should a similar abuse of power again occur on the part of a parliamentary king, he did not believe 'that the people of Ulster have lost their sturdy love of freedom nor their detestation of arbitrary power'.

But what of the native Irish themselves? At this stage the questions that logically arise are: what were the three million Irish doing in the United Kingdom in the first place; what was the source of their discontent; and what or who were the forces that made up the 'Orange Card'?

The short answer to the last question is: those who supported the Act of Union of 1800 which suppressed the Irish Parliament established in Dublin seventeen years earlier. The Parliament owed its existence to the formation of the Protestant Volunteers at Dungannon in 1782, ostensibly created merely to defend Ireland from the plagues coming from revolutionary France and America. In reality it was also used to defend the commercial interests of the ruling Protestant Ascendancy class as it was known, against the effects of English discrimination against Irish economic life as a whole, that of Protestant, Catholic and Dissenter. The Catholics suffered under the Penal Law Code, which although lately somewhat relaxed, had over the century enervated the Catholic Irish population through forbidding it property, education or advancement in government. The last category, the Presbyterians, were discriminated against for refusing to join the Established

Church and were being forced to emigrate to America.

Thus when the Dungannon Volunteers were formed, a frisson of anxiety went through the British establishment at the spectre of an Ireland growing powerful through a unity of its different factions and thus creating a commercial and strategic threat rather as though Ireland stood in the same relation to England as Cuba does to America. Mindful of such fears, although they demanded and got a parliament, the Volunteers were careful to stress their loyalty to the Crown, proclaiming at their formation that:[4]

> a claim of any body of men other than the King, Lords and Commons of Ireland to make laws for this Kingdom is unconstitutional, illegal and a grievance.

However, the Volunteers also passed a resolution drawn up by one of their founders, an enlightened Protestant landowner and orator, Henry Grattan, which declared:

> We hold the right of private judgement in matters of religion to be equally sacred in others as in ourselves...as men and as Irishmen, as Christians and as Protestants, we rejoice in the relaxation of the Penal Laws against our Roman Catholic subjects, and we conceive the measure to be fraught with the happiest of consequences to the union and prosperity of the inhabitants of Ireland ...

Throughout the coming century, it was from what might be termed the Grattan school of thought, that Catholic Ireland would derive much of its political leadership. In the immediate wake of the Volunteers' formation and the creation of the Irish Parliament, in the handsome Dublin building which now houses the Bank of Ireland, there also flowed 'the happiest of consequences'. For a brief period the independence of action and release of dynamism provided by the new Parliament created a degree of prosperity, cultural activity and social elegance that was scarcely rivalled until the coming of the contemporary 'Celtic Tiger' era. The fortunes of the Protestant Ascendancy flourished and a Catholic middle class emerged.

However, the Parliament did not address the grievances of the Catholic majority, 'that large and respectable class, the men of no property' as their champion Theobald Wolfe Tone, a Protestant lawyer, termed them. Nor were the problems of the Presbyterians solved. Accordingly, imbued with the idea of uniting 'Catholic Protestant and Dissenter', Tone became one of the leading spirits in founding and promoting another corps of Volunteers, the United Irishmen. This was largely led by Protestant idealists, the best known of whom was Lord Edward Fitzgerald, scion of a great Irish, and also a great European family. Tone did not believe in enshrining 'Kings, Lords and Commons' in the United Irishmen's republican charter, but in breaking 'the connection with England, the never-failing source of all our political evils'. He gave force to his argument that the best time to attempt such a break was when England was preoccupied with a foreign war by enlisting the aid of French forces in breaking the said evil connection.

Unfortunately for the vision of the United Irishmen, the French fleet was delayed by bureaucracy and bad weather, and the policies of the authorities goaded the rebels into a premature and ill-organised revolt in 1798. Hostile troops were billeted on the people. Militias indulged in rape, torture and murder. Joseph Holt, a Protestant Wicklow farmer who became a general in the United Irishmen's army, left a description of the incident which influenced him to take up arms. Attending a fair in Newtownmountkennedy, County Wicklow he was[5] 'sickened to witness Ancient Britons cutting the haunches and thighs off the young women for wearing green stuff petticoats'. A few Catholic United Irishmen replied in kind; for example, a Protestant church containing women and children sheltering from the rebellion was burned to the ground at Scullabogue in County Wexford, and a British army equipped with cannon and muskets thus received added incentives to slaughter opponents armed mainly with weapons such as pikes and scythes. As Thomas Pakenham has noted:[6] 'In the space of a few weeks, 30,000 people, peasants armed with pikes and pitchforks, defenceless women and children...were cut down or blown away like chaff as they charged up to the mouth of the cannon'.

Tone and Fitzgerald both died of their wounds in jail, Tone cutting his own throat so as to cheat the hangman. The Presbyterians fared so badly at the hands of the authorities that never again would they contemplate any large-scale alliance with the Catholics, and 'the men of no property' sank even deeper into poverty and despair.

In addition to 'Orange', Irish political nomenclature acquired the term 'Unionist' in the aftermath of the 1798 rebellion. The British used the uprising as an excuse to suppress Grattan's parliament and return Irish decision-taking to Westminster. As Cooke, the Under Secretary of the time, wrote in 1799:[7]

By giving the Irish a hundred members in an Assembly of six hundred and fifty they will be impotent to operate upon that Assembly, but it will be invested with Irish assent to its authority...The Union is the only means of preventing Ireland from becoming too great and too powerful.

Accordingly, an Act of Union was passed in 1800 giving legislative assent to this policy. The members of the Irish Parliament were persuaded to support the Act by inducements and pressures of all sorts, including peerages and huge bribes. The Act of Union had the effect it was intended to have. It deprived Ireland of real political power and in addition had the collateral effect of destroying the briefly flowering artistic, economic and political life of Dublin. London became the place to go for the ambitious and the energetic, the builder, the printer, the lawyer. With them departed the initiative factor and much of the energy of Irish life. The country sank into a slough of decay, mismanagement and absentee landlordism. At best, the Great Famine of the 1840s was both the inevitable and the most glaring example of the policy of depriving the Irish of the ability to address their own problems. At worst, it was an experiment in social engineering that furthered the strategic objectives of the Act of Union. Far from 'becoming too great and too powerful' Ireland lost one million of her population to starvation and a further million to emigration. Much of this emigration went to America where the Irish Catholic swamped the Presbyterian tradition and ultimately came to have a marked influence on developments in Ireland.

With the obliteration of the Irish Parliament there vanished whatever hope it contained for peaceful, evolutionary accommodation for Catholic and Protestant in Northern Ireland, and *inter alia*, through such growth, a naturally more harmonious relationship between Ireland and England. What did remain, however, in the minds of Irish Republicans, was Wolfe Tone's philosophy of breaking the relationship by striking at England when she was involved with a foreign enemy.

One of the forces which contributed greatly to both the enshrining of this belief and the bloodshed of 1798 was the Orange Order. The Order was founded after a vicious clash over land between Protestant 'Peep o Day Boys' (christened for their custom of vanishing at first light back to their homes after a night of anti-Catholic activity) and Catholic Defenders near Dan Winters' Inn in Loughall, County Armagh in the north of Ireland. The Winter home[8] today stands as an apt symbol of Orangism. It is neat, small-scale in design, respectable looking and has a violent background. Nowhere in Ireland were relations between Catholic and Protestant as bitter as in the north-eastern province of Ulster where Lowland Scottish Protestant settlers, known as 'planters', had been given most of the land formerly held by Catholics during the reign of James I. Many of these came from the English-Scottish border area and arrived in Ireland well versed in the arts of 'reiving', that is cattle-rustling, and in dealing with hostile neighbours. Along with their ruthlessness, Presbyterianism, canniness and pawky humour, they also developed a particular concept of loyalty based on the old Scottish 'banding' tradition. They would be loyal to the leader who was loyal to them. Thus, despite their fiercely proclaimed loyalty to the British Crown, there was a strong element of conditionality in that loyalty, a conditionality that would be seen in full flower in the years preceding the 1916 Rising, and it might be remarked, with equal vividness throughout the contemporary 'Troubles'.

No Irish organisation proclaimed its loyalty as loudly as did the Orangemen, who took their political hue from the Protestant William of Orange who defeated the Catholic King James II (*Seamus a Caca*, James the Shite, as the Catholic Irish termed him for his cowardice) at the Battle of the Boyne on 12 July, 1690. Symptomatic of the complexities of the Ulster issue, the battle was actually fought on 1 July under the old calendar, and the cause of King William was championed by the pope who wished to check the ambitions of King Louis of France who sponsored James II. To this day, however, the Orangemen conveniently overlook the papal contribution to the creation of their icon. Although it contained a strain of virulent anti-Catholicism, the Order had and has a substantial fraternal and benevolent component.

But, and it was a very big but indeed, it also served both as a militia and a bonding organisation for militant Protestantism, spreading to England in 1807 where the Tories, especially around Liverpool, used the movement against the Liberals. Later it would develop in America manifesting itself in such movements as the Know Nothings and the Ku Klux Klan. The Order also proved useful to employers as a device for keeping Protestant and Catholic workers from uniting for better wages and conditions.

Throughout the nineteenth century a number of unconstitutional efforts at redressing Catholic grievances were attempted, mainly led by Irish Protestants. Robert

Emmet paid for his fleeting insurrection on a public scaffold; the Young Irelanders of 1848 scarcely achieved an insurrection at all and were easily suppressed and deported to Australia and Tasmania. The largely Catholic Fenian movement seemingly achieved little in the 1860s, but, as we shall see, left a potent legacy. The greatest constitutional leader of Catholic Ireland in the nineteenth century, Daniel O'Connell, secured emancipation for his co-religionists in 1829, but died a broken man as the famine raged amidst the ruins, and indeed the consequences of the failure of his agitation for Repeal of the Union. Then in the 1870s a new movement[9] and a new policy grew up amongst Irish parliamentarians at Westminster. Led by Isaac Butt who was yet another Protestant and father of the Home Rule movement, founder of the Irish Home Rule League and a lawyer, Irish MPs attempted to obtain their objectives through obstruction, by delaying English Bills in retaliation for the English destruction of their legislative proposals for an amelioration of Irish conditions. The initiative attracted publicity and wrath in equal measure, but after a decade appeared to be a policy of activity without movement. In the ten years from 1870 to 1880 a total of twenty-eight bills aimed at improving Irish conditions fell angrily and uselessly on the floor of the House of Commons, like unpaid bills in the letter box of a bankrupt. To the Conservatives and Unionists the bribes paid to secure the passage of the Act of Union seemed to be money well spent.

Nevertheless by 1886, when Randolph Churchill played the Orange Card, the prospects for Home Rule had improved. True famine threatened once more in Ireland. There was uproar throughout the land as tenants refused to pay unjust rents and were evicted. Some enlightened Protestant thinkers in England had come to see justice in the Irish demand for an end to the Act of Union and the introduction of some measure of Home Rule. Chief amongst them was William Ewart Gladstone. While campaigning for Home Rule in Liverpool on 28 June, 1886 he said of the Act:

> There is no blacker or fouler transaction in the history of man. We used the whole civil government of Ireland as an engine of wholesale corruption…we obtained that Union against the sense of every class of the Community, by wholesale bribery and unblushing intimidation.

Gladstone was not acting solely for altruistic reasons. In Ireland the Land League, led by Michael Davitt, was agitating against landlordism and for equitable rents. The result was a series of coercive acts, agrarian outrage and a state of ebullition in rural areas where 'boycotting' was rife. The term derived from a Captain Boycott, against whom the practice was first used. Landlords who refused to reduce their rents were ostracised, or 'boycotted', neither being spoken to, served in shops, nor assisted in farm operations such as harvesting. Farmers who took land from which a tenant had been evicted were also 'boycotted'. The evicted tenants were assisted by money collected from Irish Catholics in America. But the threat of a return to famine conditions hung over the Irish countryside throughout this period and was a contributory factor to the desperation with which the peasantry waged the Land War, as it was known.

But above all, in the parliamentary war the Irish Party had

a new leader, the Protestant Wicklow landowner Charles Stewart Parnell. He still pursued Butt's policy of obstruction, but more tellingly Parnell had moulded the Irish Parliamentary Party into a formidable political machine which he used for or against either the Liberals or the Conservatives as the occasion demanded. In 1886 the Liberals needed Parnell's votes to stay in power. Apart from Davitt and Parnell, a third potent body, the Irish Republican Brotherhood or Fenian Movement, the embodiment of the Irish physical force tradition, also supported Parnell's policy. In what became known as the New Departure, the Fenians sheathed the sword and joined with the Land League in backing the Home Rule demand. In these circumstances, Home Rule appeared a certainty.

But Tory opponents of Nationalist demands did not limit themselves to merely playing the Orange Card. The papal one was played also. While attempting to maintain Protestant hegemony in Ireland, an attempt was made to enlist the pope against the Irish Catholics. It was partially successful in that it did provoke a papal response, but this rebounded on the Vatican. Pope Leo XII issued a 'papal rescript' in 1887 condemning boycotting which was badly received by the Irish, boycotters and parliamentarians alike.

The Tories then directed their attack not at a movement but a man – Parnell. As yet another Irish Coercion Act wended its way through the House of Commons in 1887, *The Times* newspaper, the organ of the Establishment, was induced to print forged letters purporting to show that Parnell was in favour of the Phoenix Park murders which had claimed the lives of a chief secretary and lord lieutenant (Cavendish and Burke), both of whom were sympathetic

towards Home Rule. The letters were subsequently proved
to be forgeries and the forger, one Richard Piggot,
committed suicide. But before this drama played out, the
Coercion Act, one of more than fifty passed since the Act of
Union, passed into law leaving Ireland virtually under a
state of martial law and at the tender mercies of Chief
Secretary Arthur Balfour, whose 'carrot and stick' policies
caused him to be remembered in Ireland as 'bloody
Balfour'. The aim of Balfour's policy was to 'kill Home Rule
with kindness', in other words, taking steps to reform the
land issue by creating a peasant proprietorship, at the same
time quelling agrarian and political disturbances with a
heavy hand.

Parnell weathered the forgery storm, but fell when the
political onslaught on him entered the sexual arena. Captain
William O'Shea sued his wife Kitty for divorce in 1889,
citing Parnell as co-respondent. O'Shea had tolerated the
liaison for several years, having lived apart from his wife
during that time in the hopes of getting his hands on her
fortune when a wealthy aunt of Kitty's died. But the money
was left in such a way that O'Shea could not touch it and in
1889 he filed a suit for divorce which he offered to drop if he
were paid £20,000 in settlement. Whether he was
encouraged by the Conservatives, in particular Joseph
Chamberlain, is to this day a debatable point. In the event
Kitty could not raise the £20,000, the divorce case provided
lurid reading and Gladstone, dependent on his non-
Conformist constituency, had to declare that so long as
Parnell remained leader of the Irish Parliamentary Party,
Home Rule could not be carried.

Instead of making a tactical retreat into the wilderness for a few years and then resuming the reins at a more propitious moment, Parnell's pride drove him to fight to remain leader. The Irish Party split into pro- and anti-Parnell factions and the strain of the in-fighting killed Parnell who died, four months after marrying Kitty, in October 1891. The Home Rule movement did not die with him but it entered a coma that was to last for approximately twenty years.

Under the leadership of John Redmond, the Irish Party's wounds were eventually healed. Patient and temperate in method and approach, Redmond had been a loyal follower of Parnell. He was from Wexford, and was MP for New Ross and later Waterford. He was also an able debater and a master of parliamentary procedure. By 1912, conditions had altered to allow the introduction of a third Home Rule Bill. Once more the Liberals were in power, and once more the Prime Minister, Herbert Asquith, was dependent on the Irish MPs. Both Asquith and his friend Augustine Birrell, the Chief Secretary for Ireland, were intellectually convinced that Home Rule was the correct policy for Ireland. The House of Lords was no longer the bulwark against Home Rule that it had been in earlier contests. As a result of the Parliament Act of 1911, Bills that passed the Commons in three consecutive sessions automatically became law whatever their lordships felt. With the disappearance of the Lords' veto it seemed that this time surely the measure must pass, particularly as the measure itself was something of a legislative mouse when compared with the mountain of discontent it had stirred up. It conceded only a very limited degree of autonomy – under the Crown – to the bi-cameral Parliament that it proposed to establish in Dublin, and reserved important powers such as defence and taxation to Westminster.

Pressure for reform of the land system culminating in the Wyndham Act of 1903 had finally created a peasant proprietorship and largely taken the Land issue out of the political equation. The southern Unionist community had lost much of its economic and political clout as many of the Anglo-Irish Ascendancy landlords had been bought out, and a relatively prosperous Catholic lower middle class had come into being.

But appearances were deceptive both in England and Ireland. In Ireland the pattern of economic and political development had diverged between the north-east and the rest of the country as the nineteenth century progressed. The overwhelming majority in the country was Catholic, but in the north-east, Protestants formed more than half the population. Economically, this section was far better off than the Catholic region. An influx of Picardy refugees gave the linen industry a boost after 1700. Both benefited from the introduction of power-spinning and weaving, and shipbuilding began in Belfast halfway through the century. All this made for the formation of capital and in Belfast in particular, something of a population explosion occurred in the wake of the new jobs. The population of 37,000 in 1821 had grown to 349,000 in 1901.

By the turn of the century it would not be altogether inaccurate to think of industrialised Ireland as lying largely in what are now referred to by Nationalists as the Six Counties: Antrim, Down, Armagh, Derry, Fermanagh and Tyrone, and the rest consisting mainly of a large farm and Guinness's Brewery in Dublin. Industrialisation, being Protestant-financed and controlled, did not merely heighten the north-east's differences from the rest of the country;

they made Belfast part of an economic unit centred on British cities such as Manchester, Liverpool and Glasgow. Belfast looked to and traded with these areas and thought in terms of building up northern cities like Derry and Portadown rather than investing in Dublin. Belfast became the magnet not only for Protestants but also for many impoverished Catholics seeking jobs that the Protestants had created.

The contest for jobs was thus superimposed on older conflicts arising from the Plantation, heightening the anxieties of the descendants of the British and Protestant settlers in Ulster who saw themselves very much as settlers do in any part of the world who live on land taken from an indigenous people: constantly in danger of being swept away by a vengeful tide of the dispossessed.

In England, however, the Conservatives were less concerned with the growth of Irish Catholic power than they were about the loss of their own. As an historian of Unionism, Patrick Buckland has written: 'Unionists, furious with frustration at their continued exclusion from power, were thus willing to adopt almost any means to defeat the Liberals and return to office'. The Orange Card had played its part in ensuring almost unbroken Tory rule between 1886 and the end of 1905. However the Party lost power between 1892 and 1895, again in 1906, and more importantly, in 1911. The following year, on 11 April, 1912, Prime Minister Asquith, a convinced Home Ruler, and like Gladstone, dependent on the Irish MPs, moved the third and this time what seemed to be an inevitably successful Home Rule Bill in the House of Commons. The Bill was rejected twice by the House of Lords but on its third circuit it was passed by the House of Commons on 25 May, 1914 by a majority of seventy-seven votes. In normal circumstances the measure would then have received the royal assent and passed into law. But where Ireland was concerned the abnormal had become the norm to the Tories. They resorted to extra-parliamentary methods and brought the Orange Card into play once more. Once again Ulster was told that she would be right to fight.

In April 1912, three days before Asquith introduced the first reading of the Home Rule Bill, the Conservative leader Bonar Law had presided over what was described as 'the wedding of Protestant Ulster with the Conservative and Unionist Party' at a demonstration in Balmoral, a suburb of Belfast. Prayers were said by the Primate of All Ireland and the Moderator of the Presbyterian Church in the presence of seventy English, Scottish and Welsh MPs, while overhead flapped a Union Jack measuring some 48 feet by 25 feet, said to be the largest ever woven. Bonar Law recalled the successful defiance of the Protestants who withstood the Catholic Siege of Derry during the Williamite campaign, saying:[10]

> Once again you hold the pass, the pass for the Empire. You are a besieged city. The timid have left you; your Lundys have betrayed you; but you have closed your gates. The Government have erected by their Parliament Act a boom against you to shut you off from the help of the British people. You will burst that boom. That help will come, and when the crisis is over, men will say to you in words not unlike those used by Pitt – you have saved yourselves by your exertions, and you will save the Empire by your example.

Those words spoken on Easter Tuesday 1912 were to have a significant bearing on what would befall Dublin at a subsequent Easter in 1916. The Conservative Party leader followed up his Balmoral utterances the following July, the month in which Orange fervour traditionally reaches its perfervid peak. Speaking at Blenheim on 24 July, he delivered what Asquith described as a 'reckless rodomontade, a declaration of war against Constitutional Government' and a 'furnishing forth the complete grammar of anarchy':

We regard the Government as a revolutionary committee which has seized upon despotic power by fraud. In our opposition to them we shall not be guided by the considerations or bound by the restraints which would influence us in an ordinary constitutional struggle. We shall take the means, whatever means seem to us most effective, to deprive them of the despotic power which they have usurped and compel them to appeal to the people whom they have deceived. They may, perhaps they will, carry their Home Rule Bill through the House of Commons and I repeat here that there are things stronger than parliamentary majorities…Before I occupied the position which I now fill in the party I said that, in my belief, if an attempt were made to deprive these men of their birthright – as part of a corrupt parliamentary bargain – they would be justified in resisting such an attempt by all means in their power, *including force* [author's emphasis]. I said it then, and I repeat now with a full sense of the responsibility which attaches to my position, that, in my opinion, if such an attempt is made, I can imagine no length of resistance to which Ulster can go in which I should not be prepared to support them, and in which, in my belief, they would not be supported by the overwhelming majority of the British people.

The leaders of the 'lengths of resistance' to which Ulster was prepared to go were Edward Carson, a former Crown prosecutor, Unionist MP for Trinity College, Dublin and leader of the Irish Unionist MPs at Westminster, and his lieutenant James Craig, MP for East Down, appropriately enough in the Irish context, a millionaire whiskey distiller. By 1912 Carson's forensic prowess had brought him success at the English Bar after a career in Ireland largely built on the premise that the term 'Irish Catholic Nationalist' was the long version of the word 'defendant'. Arthur Balfour once wrote:[11]

I made Carson and he made me. I've told you how no one had courage. Everyone right up to the top was trembling...Carson had nerve, however. I sent him all over the place, getting convictions, we worked together.

Now, having based his career on upholding the wishes of British governments, Carson turned his talents to flouting them. His activities included the preparations for a provisional government to rule 'Ulster', gun-running and the announcement to the world on 19 September, 1912 of the Ulster Covenant inspired by the Old Scottish Covenant.[12] The symbolism of the Dan Winter cottage was heightened by Orange apologists who argued that the announcement of the Covenant was necessary because it provided an opportunity not to promote civil disorder but to impose discipline. The summer, and in particular the marching month of July, had been punctuated by several outbursts of disorder. Five days before the launching of the Covenant, a football match between Catholic Celtic and the Protestant Linfield became a battleground in which such aids as knives and revolvers were vigorously employed to enhance the enjoyment of the beautiful game. It was against this background that Carson read the Covenant from the steps of Craig's family seat, Craigavon. It said:

Being convinced in our consciences that Home Rule would be disastrous to the material well-being of Ulster as well as the whole of Ireland, subversive of our civil and religious freedom, destructive of our citizenship, and perilous to the unity of the Empire, we, whose names are underwritten, men of Ulster, loyal subjects of His Gracious Majesty King George V, humbly relying on the God whom our fathers in days of stress and trial confidently trusted, do hereby pledge ourselves in solemn covenant throughout this our time of threatened calamity to stand by one another in defending for ourselves and our children our cherished position of equal citizenship in the United Kingdom, and in using all means which may be found necessary to defeat the present conspiracy to set up a Home Rule Parliament in Ireland. And in the event of such a parliament being forced upon us we further solemnly and mutually pledge ourselves to refuse to recognise its authority. In sure confidence that God will defend the right we hereto subscribe our names. And further, we individually declare that we have not already signed this covenant. God save the King.

The Covenant was signed by a total of 471,414 people, including civil servants, soldiers and police in uniform. Carson boasted afterwards that the Government 'dared not touch one of them'. By way of putting muscle behind those signatures, the Orangemen also began making open military preparations. A Protestant Volunteer Force, formed from the signatories of the Covenant, which sprang up in the wake of the Covenant's signing, displayed the Orangeman's penchant for keeping within the law while taking steps to break it. Carson took advantage of provision of the law whereby if the signatures of two Justices of the Peace were obtained for the area under their jurisdiction, drilling and other militaristic preparations could take place 'provided that the object was to render citizens more efficient for the purpose of maintaining the Constitution of the United Kingdom as established'.

Throughout this uproar the Crimes Act which the Piggot forgery case helped to facilitate was still in operation and could have been invoked as vigorously as it was against Nationalists. But this was not done. During September 1913, for example, a great series of Unionist parades and meetings took place throughout the north-east. Carson announced that a government would be set up which would take over the control of the province on the day that the Home Rule Act became law. 'I am told it will be illegal,' he declared openly at Newry on the 7th, and went on:

> Of course it will. Drilling is illegal...the Volunteers are illegal and the Government know they are illegal, and the Government dare not interfere with them...Don't be afraid of illegalities.

On 24 September, the Ulster Unionist Council, without the formality of any election, resolved itself into the 'Central Authority of the Provisional Government of Ulster'. Sir Edward Carson became chairman of the Central Authority and the members included Captain Craig, the Duke of Abercorn and the Marquis of Londonderry. A legal assessor was appointed – the Right Hon. James Campbell, KC, MP; various committees were appointed and a military council was set up. Carson said of his policy that he did not 'care two pence whether it was treason or not'.

He did not have to care. The Ulster Volunteers could rely on far greater support than local magistrates. Wild and swirling Tory utterances filled the air. At Ballyclare in County Antrim (on 20 September, 1913) F. E. Smith, KC, Conservative Member for a Liverpool constituency, later to be made an Attorney General of England and the Earl of Birkenhead, declared on behalf of the Conservatives that the moment Home Rule was made law: 'we will say to our followers in England, "to your tents, O Israel!"'. They would be ready, he averred, 'to risk the collapse of the whole body politic to prevent this monstrous crime'. The Duchess of Somerset also declared herself amongst the Israelites. She wrote to Carson in January 1914:

This is to assure you of our unfailing support and to implore you to take all care of yourself – so as to save Ireland...

The day that the first shot is fired in Ireland – I shall have my complete ambulance started and ready – 2 medical men, 2 surgeons, 6 trained nurses, and 32 orderlies – I have also undertaken to house 100 women and children from Ulster –

The Duke and I will both come over to give all the help we can...

This little letter is just a note of encouragement for I know how depressed you must be at times but in such a noble cause! It is worth while and it's the weakness of our rulers at the present time who have helped the Traitors and little Englishmen to bring their evil doings to this impasse...

The country will follow you now and we shall all help you to see this thing through and this vile government will go out and perhaps a reign of peace will come...

The duchess was not alone. Support also came from Bonar Law, who apart from his experience in Ulster as a son of the manse during his father's time as a minister, was heavily influenced by Lord and, particularly, Lady Londonderry, who acted as his London political hostess. The Carsonite camp also included figures such as Lord Milner, Waldorf Astor, Lord Rothschild, Lord Ivy, the Duke of Bedford, Sir Edward Elgar and Rudyard Kipling. Milner, the former High Commissioner for South Africa, wrote to Carson on 9 December, 1913:

...there must very soon, certainly in less than a year, be what would be technically a 'rebellion' in Ulster. It would be a disaster of the first magnitude if that 'rebellion', which would really be the uprising of unshakeable principle and devoted patriotism – of loyalty to the Empire and the flag – were to fail. But it must fail unless we can paralyse the arm which might be raised to strike you.

In the event, this sort of thinking would help to provoke not an Orange rebellion in Belfast but a green one in Dublin. The imperialists saw nothing incongruous in their fomenting of 'loyal Protestant' rebellion as opposed to the treacherous Catholic variety, as Kipling made clear in a poem for the Unionists which appeared in the *Morning Post:*[13]

The blood our fathers spilt
Our love our toils our pains,
Are counted us for guilt,
And only bind our chains.
Before an Empire's eyes,
The traitor claims his price.
What need of further lies?
We are the sacrifice.

We know the war prepared
On every peaceful home,
We know the hells declared
For such as serve not Rome –
The terror, threats, and dread
In market, hearth, and field –
We know, when all is said,
We perish if we yield.

Believe, we dare not boast,
Believe, we do not fear –
We stand to pay the cost
In all that men hold dear.
What answer from the North?
One law, one land, one throne.
If England drive us forth
We shall not fall alone.

As Asquith commented, Bonar Law had introduced a new style of rancour and an anarchical grammar into British politics. He and the other Unionist spokespersons also introduced two factors which remain with us to this day.

One of these is the custom of referring to the six industrialised and Unionist-dominated counties of north-eastern Ireland as 'Ulster', whereas the term properly applies to the historic province of Ulster that includes the counties of Donegal (the most northerly county), Cavan and Monaghan. The second factor is the concept of partition. This was first proposed on 11 June, 1912 by a Liberal Unionist, T. C. R. Agar-Robartes, an MP for a Cornish constituency. He put forward an amendment to the Home Rule Bill proposing that four of the north-eastern counties, Antrim, Armagh, Down and Derry, be excluded from the Bill. This was purely a tactical manoeuvre, known to be unacceptable to the Irish Parliamentary Party, and was put forward as a parliamentary figleaf in an attempt to make the Unionists appear reasonable and open to compromise. Nine years later, however, it would form the basis of the compromise which yielded the Irish Treaty, the two states of modern Ireland and more than eighty years of sporadic violence.

The irony of the situation was that the atmosphere of threat and defiance of parliamentary democracy was not unwelcome to the people it was ultimately directed at, the leaders of the Irish Republican Brotherhood, who would ultimately stage the 1916 revolution. These men were neither enamoured of Home Rule, nor of the ameliorative legislation which had been enacted. To them these were mere crumbs from the rich man's political table. They aspired not to an Ireland with a degree of autonomy under the Crown, but to a free, independent Republic fashioned on the principles of Wolfe Tone. Theirs was not a large constituency until Carson and the Conservatives changed the picture. A highly placed member of the Irish Republican Brotherhood, Piaras Beaslai, who helped to plan and to participate in the Rising, penned the following description of how the Nationalist revolutionaries viewed Carson's eruption on to the political stage:[14]

In an Ireland doped into an unlimited patience, and credulity, an unlimited confidence in its Party Leaders, and in the British Liberal government, and a confident expectation of Home Rule, came Sir Edward Carson to save the situation for the physical force party. He, more than any man, is responsible for the events which have created the Irish Free State. He defied law, appealed to force; he preached the doctrines which led to the founding of the Irish Volunteers – and the amazed Irish people, with their pathetic faith in the infallibility of their Party leaders, and the honesty of the British Government, saw that Government recoil before the bluff of the 'Ulster Volunteers'. They found threats of physical resistance by a minority accepted as a successful argument against justice to a majority. They found that the rifles and parading of the 'Ulster Volunteers' were jeopardising the long-expected Home Rule Act. Here was the opportunity of the IRB [the Irish Republican Brotherhood].

At first sight the Ireland and in particular the Dublin of which Beaslai wrote did not appear to provide much opportunity for the IRB. At the time of the 1916 Rising, the actual form of government in Ireland was carried out by what was known as the Executive which controlled the army, the police and the civil service. There was a Lord Lieutenant, a Chief Secretary and an Under Secretary. The first two of the three were politicians, the third a civil servant. At the time of the Rising, the long-serving Chief Secretary, Augustine Birrell, was a member of the Cabinet. But the Lord Lieutenant, Lord Wimborne, who was allegedly responsible for the government, was not. Wimborne might propose, but Birrell disposed. The Under Secretary was Sir Matthew Nathan, an able and vastly experienced administrator. Were he given to premonitions, a shudder might well have convulsed him as he addressed his first task in Ireland. It was to arrange for a transfer to the colonies of a police officer, Assistant Commissioner Harrell, who was made the scapegoat for the Bachelors Walk incident we will encounter later. Nathan himself would be made a scapegoat over another far greater incident to which Bachelors Walk was a contributory factor – the 1916 Rising.

In fact the Ireland of the time could hardly have been administered by ten Matthew Nathans. From the outside, looking at the opulence of the Vice-regal Lodge and Dublin Castle, and the confidence of the splendidly accoutred British officers, the place seemed safe, snobbish and secure, as depicted, for instance, in the pages of *A Drama in Muslin* by George Moore.

Piaras Beaslai, even after the Rising, would write that Dublin was a hot bed of Loyalism and that the IRB could make no headway against Birrell's softly, softly policy. Birrell read widely in Irish history and worked assiduously to make Home Rule possible. He contemplated neither Partition nor a cave-in to the Carsonites. He put through fifty-five Bills dealing with Ireland on subjects as diverse as housing, land and the creation of a national university. He actively tried to increase the role of Irish Catholics in their own country, and for this inevitably became a figure of execration for the Orangemen. On the other hand, the IRB viewed Birrell's policy as merely being a variant on the long-standing British governmental policy of rewarding:

> ...their supporters in Ireland (quaintly called 'loyalists') with place and power. The enlightened Liberal Administration introduced a new system of buying up Nationalists. Positions in the gift of the Government began to be secured by the patronage of the Irish Party.

Beaslai sourly commented that 'The astute Mr Birrell, the ablest of Irish Chief Secretaries, flattered the Irish people by witty speeches and declined to imprison popular agitators'. Yet despite Beaslai's criticism of him, Birrell realised that Ireland was fundamentally distrustful of the English connection. 'It is not,' he said in 1907, 'that Dublin Castle is a sink of jobbery or corruption. But it is, to use a familiar expression, "switched off" from the current of National life and feeling. No pulse of real life beats in its breast. The main current of Irish thought as they surge around its walls, pass almost unheeded.' He judged ruefully and truly that: 'Nobody in Ireland, north or south, save a handful of officials, was, or ever had been, loyal to England in the true sense of the word.' One wonders if Birrell himself fully understood how that Irish interpretation of the word 'loyalty' was arrived at. Another view of how the Castle operated, prepared for Michael Collins by Castle civil servant Thomas Markham, also had a certain jaundiced validity:[15]

The British system was based on:
(a) The grasp of human weakness and vanity.
(b) A correct appreciation of the value and use of duplicity and Pecksniffianism.
(c) A clear conception of the truth that success in governing depends on well-contrived antagonisms in the economic and social structure of the state.

A new Chief Secretary is powerless to alter the system fundamentally, or even 'materially'. Yet all departures (in policy) went to him. All staff are vetted by the police with exhaustive descriptions of family tree in all its hues and activities.

Belfast staff is very carefully selected as to loyalty. Numerical strength makes it a Staff-in-Waiting prepared to work for the whole Irish service if and when the opportunity arises.

Dealing with police and politics were the pivotal props of the system...The Royal Irish Constabulary, organised in Counties, Districts...During his training his vanity, ignorance and intelligence were each subjected to the treatment designed to make the British Government his servant and his God. The RIC had something to do with every phase of governmental activity.

The constable records everything in his diary. What he frightens from the child and coaxes from the *cailin*. What he hears, sees, infers. The sergeant transfers the constable's report, never abbreviating. It is not his part to select. The policeman moves in a social atmosphere, he writes down everything, gossipy servants, what the RIC pensioner says. A 'Someone' whose name is never written down. He's a 'reliable source'. He could be the publican. The rail spy could be the inspector. He frequently is.

The road to the Castle is paved with anonymous letters, deriving from the besetting Irish sin, jealousy. The depth and widespread nature of this treachery would make a good Irishman despair. The local Loyalist could have a good post and be merely a disreputable spotter...what was said at a Volunteer meeting; where arms were kept; the eavesdropping prison warder; the opening of letters in the post. Ambiguity and elasticity are the marked features of the system enabling the Administration to sanction in Belfast what it refused in Dublin. The exact standard of Irish morality, public and private, was taken, and rule measured in accordance. Ideology was ignored.

Markham, who was writing a few years after 1916, judged that the Nationalists were in reality 'kicking down a rotten door'. True, the trains ran on time and the postal service was far better then than it is at the time of writing; an inevitable consequence, one might say, of a state's revolutionary birth occurring in a post office. But as Birrell correctly noted, there was a gulf between the governed and the governing. In Dublin and throughout the country in Catholic areas, there was a heightened consciousness of being Irish. Whether this consciousness took the form of sporting, literary, political or even military activity, it was clearly distinctive. The energy of the Irish, their Celtic apartness from both the English and the bowler-hatted Orangemen could be seen in the plays of Yeats, Synge and Lady Gregory put on in the

Abbey Theatre which they had founded. A survivor of 1916, speaking in propagandist rather than literary terms, once remarked to me wonderingly of Yeats: 'The bloody auld bastard! You'd think by tradition he'd be a proper old Unionist, but be God he was a great help to us!' A host of writers, poets and polemicists, George Russell, D. P. Moran, the editor of the *Leader*, and above all, Arthur Griffith, poured forth their individual visions of Ireland. Griffith was born in Dublin in 1872 and educated by the Christian Brothers. He left school early to work in a Dublin newspaper office. He supported Parnell and when his leadership ended, Griffith emigrated to South Africa. At the outbreak of the Boer War he returned to Dublin and began work as a journalist. He founded Sinn Fein (We Ourselves) in 1905. Two of his works, *Thomas Davis: Thinker and Teacher*, and in particular, *The Resurrection of Hungary – a Parallel for Ireland*, became standard Nationalist texts.

Griffith noted that Hungary had won its independence by refusing to send members to the imperial parliament in Vienna, rejecting its claims to legislate for Hungary's internal affairs. He advocated a dual monarchy for Ireland, similar to that of Austro-Hungary, with two separate legislatures for England and Ireland; in effect a restoration of Grattan's parliament. In economic matters he was a disciple of Friedrich List, the German protectionist, and advocated tariffs as a means of building up Irish industries.

The Gaelic League founded by Douglas Hyde, and the Gaelic Athletic Association established by Michael Cusack, were recreating and repopularising the Irish language and Irish games, notably Gaelic football and the incredibly skilful and dangerous sport of hurling. It was via these two organisations that most of the ardent young Nationalists of that time first passed through the portals of revolution, although neither of the two bodies' founders created them for that purpose. Hyde, in particular, who was a Protestant, academic, poet and playwright, was horrified when he discovered that the IRB was manipulating the Gaelic League for its own purposes. Some of the artistic depictions, the imagery used to convey this rediscovered Celticism, was wishful thinking based on the familiar syndrome of a Nationalist feeling in an era of colonialism, expressing itself in terms of an imagined Golden Age of the past. Legendary High Kings, beautiful queens, harps and round towers, all bound up with tales of the days when Ireland was the Land of Saints and Scholars, found their way into revivalist culture.

The 'Celtic Dawn' is the term used to describe all these happenings and it was an accurate enough description of what occurred at many levels in Irish society. As injustices were rectified and some educational and economic opportunities created, there was a recommencement of some of the growth and cultural expansion that had been halted by the Act of Union. As a result, there was an unusually high population of young people in the country, young Catholics who would otherwise have had to emigrate. But while there was some economic outlet, where was the political outlet for this younger generation? In life, in nature, a tree, a family, a business or a political development either grows or it dies. Thus it was with the natural, constitutional, organic movement towards self-government in Ireland. The Dawn was rising on a deceptively calm Nationalist landscape. Under the surface, the effects of the political stultification caused by the manipulation of power from outside Dublin, the nominal capital of the country, were beginning to be felt. Although Dublin didn't have industries, it had all the evils of the slumlands associated with industrial Britain. Dublin's slums were some of the worst in Europe.[16]

In 1910 a survey found that in the slums 20,000 families were living in one room each. Infant mortality was 142 per thousand compared with 103 in London. The Poor Law Commission's Report for the same year states that among the 1254 families investigated, weekly wages ranged from a maximum of £3, down to a minimum of five shillings, the average being £1 2s 2d a week. In these conditions, crime and drunkenness flourished. The national average in Ireland for crimes like forgery, rape and murder was 21.02 per ten thousand, but in Dublin it was 100 per ten thousand. Twenty-two Dublin public houses were kept under observation for a fortnight and it was found that 46,574 women and 27,999 children patronised them in that period – and not merely because most of them sold groceries as well. Insanity frequently caused by drinking methylated spirits or turpentine was estimated at 63.5 per thousand.

These conditions created one of the flints – the Irish Citizen Army – that helped to spark off the 1916 Rising. The Army was founded to defend strikers from police brutality during the great Dublin lockout of 1913. This was a battle between the forces of capitalism led by William Martin Murphy at the head of the Dublin employers, and the workers led by the mesmeric trade unionist James Larkin. The lockout ended in defeat for the workers and Larkin departed for America. But his colleague James Connolly, who with Larkin had founded the Irish Transport and General Workers' Union, remained in Dublin with his tiny Citizen Army operating from the union's headquarters, Liberty Hall.

Connolly was born in County Monaghan in 1870. His parents moved to Edinburgh where he started work at the age of eleven. He educated himself by reading, married and returned to Ireland as a socialist organiser. He printed and edited the first Irish socialist paper, *The Workers' Republic*. He worked in America from 1903 to 1910 as an organiser for the Independent Workers of the World, the 'Wobblies', founded an Irish Socialist Federation and edited *The Harp*. He was a staunch believer in the emancipation of women and made Constance Markievicz (*née* Gore-Booth) an officer in the Citizen Army. She was born to the 'Big House', daughter of a Protestant landowner at Lissadell in County Sligo in 1868. Her sister was the poet, Eva Gore-Booth. Both were beautiful and talented, moving Yeats to describe them and the destiny that befell Constance as follows:

> *Two girls in silk kimonos, both*
> *Beautiful, one a gazelle*
>
> *The older is condemned to death,*
> *Pardoned, drags out lonely years*
> *Conspiring amongst the ignorant.*

At one stage in her career Constance had led an active social life, studied painting and produced plays. She married a Polish count, Casimir Dunin Markievicz and founded *Fianna Eireann*, the IRB's, and later the IRA's Boy Scout

Movement. The assistance she rendered the strikers by working in Liberty Hall's soup kitchens during the great lockout persuaded Connolly to appoint her an officer in his Citizen Army. An old nun who had lived through the period described to me once how the poor saw her. Constance was speaking at an election meeting, after the Rising, during which she made frequent references to what Sinn Fein intended to do in the Dail (the Irish Parliament in which she was appointed Minister for Labour, the first woman cabinet minister in Europe). After listening to the cultivated voice's frequent references to the 'Dawll' one Dublin 'aul one' turned to another and remarked audibly: 'The doll! Ah, will you look at her blouse. She's lovely. She's a real doll herself!'

Connolly was a man of international outlook, his nationalism and his socialism were fused together in outrage at the appalling slum conditions that British rule had produced in Ireland. His enthusiasm for a protest in arms was such that in January of 1916 the IRB kidnapped him and after some days of parley during which Markievicz threatened to release him by force, they co-opted him into their councils to stop him going ahead with only the support of the Citizen Army, which would have brought down an avalanche on all of them. This Army was founded to defend the workers from police brutality during the lockout at the instigation of Captain Jack White, the son of a British field-marshal. White had won a DSO for his services to the Crown during the Boer War. Another prominent Boer War figure who would train, fight and die with the insurgents was Major John MacBride who had led his own Irish, pro-Boer Brigade during the conflict. He was the estranged husband of Maude Gonne, the woman that Yeats loved.

The apparently unassailably controlling political leaders of the day, John Redmond and his colleagues John Dillon, Joseph Devlin and William O'Brien, were in fact dangerously removed from the country, locked into the parliamentary battle at Westminster, influenced by 'the tone of the house'; the insidious tendency to see things Irish in an English light. And well out of sight of that light there was the minuscule Irish Republican Brotherhood (IRB) to whom the Carsonites now proffered the opportunity to act as the detonator of Irish Nationalism.

As Europe moved inexorably to war and England seemingly towards civil war over the Home Rule issue, there occurred an incident which more than any other helped to convince elements within the larger Nationalist Ireland community that Home Rule might not be achieved solely by constitutional means after all. This was the Curragh mutiny[17] affair which appeared to demonstrate that Bonar Law's 'overwhelming majority' included the British Army. By March 1914 the progress of the Home Rule Bill at Westminster had reached a stage where, at least according to rumour, the Liberal Government intended to use the Army to curb the activities of the drilling Orangemen. The Army was to have moved troops from the Curragh in County Kildare in the south, to Ulster in the north in order to guard military installations and other strategic strong points. However, on 20 March, 1914, the Commander-in-Chief in Ireland, General Sir Arthur Paget, telegraphed the War Office that General Hubert Gough, an Ulster man, and fifty-seven officers of the Third Cavalry Brigade had stated that they would prefer dismissal to the prospect of moving north. Earlier in the month, a British version of the Ulster

Covenant had been launched in the British press by Lord Alfred Milner. This stated:

> I…of…earnestly convinced that the claim of the government to carry the Home Rule bill without submitting it to the judgement of the nation is contrary to the spirit of our constitution, do hereby solemnly declare that if that bill is passed I shall hold myself justified in taking or supporting any action that may be effective to prevent it being put into operation, and more particularly to prevent the armed forces of the Crown being used to deprive the people of Ulster of their rights as citizens of the United Kingdom.

Clearly Gough and his colleagues agreed with the passage 'I shall hold myself justified in taking or supporting any action that may be effective to prevent it being put into operation' particularly insofar as 'the armed forces of the Crown' were concerned. More importantly, powerful figures in the establishment were prepared to manipulate Gough's defiance after he was summoned to London for a confrontation with the Minister for War, Colonel John Seely. Gough emerged not to face the prospect of a court martial but with a document of capitulation which he had wrung out of Seely with the aid of the Director of Military Operation, General (later Field Marshal) Sir Henry Wilson. The last paragraph was in fact dictated by Wilson and appeared on the document in Gough's own handwriting. It stated:

> I understand the reading of the last paragraph to be that the troops under our command will not be called upon to

enforce the present Home Rule Bill on Ulster, and that we can so assure our officers.

The import of that piece of paper became apparent a month later. In view of the dangerous situation in Ireland (as we shall shortly see, the Nationalists had taken a leaf out of the Orangemen's book and begun to organise), a ban on arms importation had been announced the previous December. But during the night of 24–5 April, 1914, the Ulster Volunteers landed 35,000 rifles and five million rounds of ammunition from the *Clydevalley* at Larne Harbour. In the process police and customs officials were held up, but the Army did not intervene. The *Clydevalley* weapons were then loaded into several hundred waiting motorcars and transported around the province to safe hiding places, again without any interference from the authorities.

It is time now to examine the forces that lay behind the decision to organise a Nationalist volunteer force in reaction to the foregoing events – the Irish Republican Brotherhood or Fenian Movement as it was popularly known. All the revolutionary traditions of Wolfe Tone and the United Irishmen and of the various separatist leaders thrown up in earlier centuries of dispossession and war were distilled into the philosophy of the Fenians, named after the legendary Irish version of the Japanese Samurai. But the IRB, though some of them acquired mythic proportion, were far from being mythical figures. They were real-life, practical conspirators whose movement came into being in New York and Dublin in 1858.

James Stephens, who had taken part in the abortive uprising of 1848, formally launched the movement on St

Patrick's Day on the basis of an £80 donation from fellow survivors of 1848 then living in the US, where its principal moving spirit was John O'Mahony. The Movement was modelled on the revolutionary societies which Stephens had encountered while living in Paris after the 1848 Rebellion. It was organised on a circle basis in which each circle or cell contained only one person who knew who the members of the next circle were and so on. Sean Cronin, an historian of the Fenians, has correctly said of Fenianism that:[18]

> Its victories were few, yet Fenianism remained a weapon of the Irish poor wherever they were; radical in outlook, fiercely non-sectarian, and because of the anathemas of the bishops – anti-clerical. Fenians shouted defiance from the dock, challenged their jailers and walked erect to the gallows. The rank and file, not the leaders, saved Fenianism.

Cronin could have been describing the character of the 1916 Volunteers. From the outset the Fenians were riddled with informers and bedevilled by splits, but it soon became a force to be reckoned with in Irish affairs. In 1865 the American wing of the Movement established what some regarded as a government-in-exile. John O'Mahony was its president. It had an army drawn from the Irish who had fought on both sides of the American Civil War, a senate, a house of delegates and a cabinet. In the eyes of O'Mahony and those who thought like him, the Irish Republic was 'now virtually established'. However, a section of the cabinet did not think like him and wanted to devote the Movement's energies to an invasion of Canada, which would put pressure on the British to negotiate the independence of Ireland. The Fenians split and the upshot was not one but two attempts to invade Canada.[19]

One faction led by O'Mahony plotted to take control of Campo Bello Island, a British holding off the coast of Maine; the other to invade Canada itself. The Campo Bello initiative was scotched by British and American co-operation, but the Canadian invasion went ahead later that year, in June 1866. The Fenian leader, Colonel John O'Neill, at the head of a force of 600 men achieved some success, capturing Fort Erie and defeating a British force at the Battle of Ridgeway. However, bereft of reinforcements, O'Neill's force, significantly described as the Irish Republican Army (IRA), retreated back to American soil after only two days and surrendered to the Americans.

The Fenians also planned an invasion and an uprising in Ireland itself the following year. But the police were forewarned and the rebellion was scotched, lasting for little more than a day. However, bomb plots, rescues and failed rescues continued to keep the name of the IRB before the Irish public for decades. In an attempt to rescue the Fenian leader, Colonel Kelly, in Manchester, a policeman was accidentally shot and three Manchester Fenians were hanged as a result. The names of the three, Allen, Larkin and O'Brien, passed into the Pantheon of Irish martyrdom, remembered in one of the most famous 'scaffold songs', *The Smashing of the Van*. One of the most spectacular exploits of the Fenians was to rescue a number of Fenians from Fremantle Jail in Western Australia, aboard the *Catalpa* in 1875. At the time of writing, one of the biggest pubs in Perth is called 'The Fenians'. The men sailed back to a hero's welcome in America where there was a large Irish presence created by the famine.

The principal Fenian off-shoot was the *Clan na Gael*, which acted 'in concert with the IRB' in Ireland and which at the time of the 1916 Rising was led by John Devoy, an old Fenian who had joined the French Foreign Legion to receive military training. He had supported 'the New Departure' of throwing the Fenian Movement behind Parnell, and when this failed, succeeded ultimately in uniting the various feuding factions of the Clan and the IRB in Atlantic City, New Jersey in July 1900 behind the demand for an Irish Republic to be achieved by physical force if necessary. The IRB in Ireland, however, seemed most unlikely to provide that force. It existed in a semi-moribund state, led principally by John O'Leary and Charles J. Kickham, two men who were better known for their literary abilities than their Fenianism. It was the presence of figures like these in the movement which led the poet W. B. Yeats to join them. But insofar as militarism was concerned, keeping alive the memory of the dead and/or attending funerals appeared to be the IRB's principal activity.

However, in the early years of the twentieth century this began to change. Mindful of Grattan's example, two Nationalists, Catholic Denis McCullough and Quaker Bulmer Hobson, founded an organisation called the Dungannon Clubs in Belfast. It preached separatism, attacked recruiting to the British Army, Navy or police force, and in a series of pamphlets, preached Republicanism and extended the hand of friendship to the Orangemen. From 1905 onward the Dungannon Clubs began to intertwine with the Sinn Fein Movement. Hobson and McCullough

readily agreed with Griffith that there was nothing to be
gained by putting faith in 'any such myths as English justice
or English mercy' or by the 'useless, degrading and
demoralising policy' of the Irish Party at Westminster.
Griffith inverted the argument of Cooke more than a
century earlier, thundering:[20]

> Ireland has maintained a representation of 103 men in the
> English Parliament for 108 years...The 103 Irishmen are
> faced with 567 foreigners...Ten years hence the majority of
> Irishmen will marvel they once believed that the proper
> battle-ground for Ireland was one chosen and filled by
> Ireland's enemies.

Although numerically small, the generic title 'Sinn Fein'
came to be applied to those who supported Irish
independence, and Griffith's general policy as opposed to
the Irish Parliamentary Party's dull, dogged march towards
Home Rule. However, under the Sinn Fein umbrella there
was a considerable divide between the socialist James
Connolly and the capitalist-minded Griffith who
disapproved of strikes. The Dungannon Clubs' Republican
theorists also found fault with Griffith's monarchist ideas.
Above all, where the IRB was concerned, Griffith suffered
the supreme drawback of being a constitutionalist, not a
physical force man, although he ran a newspaper called *The
United Irishman*, named after the 1840s newspaper of
Young Irelander leader John Mitchell which had preached
Tone's doctrines. In 1907, a figure much more to the
Dungannon school's way of thinking arrived in Dublin.

Thomas James Clarke was born in England of Irish

parents in 1858, spent his childhood in South Africa until the age of ten, then lived in Dungannon in Ulster until he went to America at the age of twenty-one. Joining the *Clan na Gael*, he returned to Ireland as a dynamiter, the precursor of the Provisional IRA's London bombers. He was imprisoned for fifteen years under conditions which drove many of his fellows to death or insanity. Released in 1889, he went to America before returning to Ireland where he opened a small tobacconist's shop in Parnell Street in Dublin. In 1901 he married Kathleen Daly, daughter of fellow prisoner, Fenian leader John Daly and sister to one of Clarke's principal officers in 1916, Ned Daly.

He was co-opted on to the Supreme Council of the IRB which proceeded to take two important steps. Firstly, it appointed Sean MacDermott as a full-time organiser throughout the country. MacDermott (Sean MacDiarmada) was born in County Leitrim. He spent his early years in Scotland and in America before returning to Ireland and became the most important IRB organiser and recruiter despite being lame and weakened by polio. He was an active member of the Gaelic League, the Gaelic Athletic Association and of Sinn Fein as well as being editor and manager of the IRB paper. The founding of this paper, *Irish Freedom*, was the IRB's second important move. *Irish Freedom* expounded the full unexpurgated Republican doctrine. In 1911 the IRB split over the ostensible issue of control of the newspaper; the real issue was the clash of the generations between the Hobson, McCullough, MacDermott wing of the IRB, and their elders, Fred Allan, John O'Hanlon and P. T. Daly. Clarke supported the younger men.

The strength[21] of the Clarke faction was estimated at a convention of the Clan in Atlantic City in 1912 as being 1660 in Ireland and 367 in Britain. The youth wing of the Movement, *Fianna Eireann*, led by Countess Markievicz and Liam Mellowes, was said to be 1000 strong and the circulation of *Irish Freedom* at 6000 copies a month. A sum of $2000 a year was allocated by the convention to further development in Ireland. These figures give an idea of the relative strengths of the forces which would be thought of as rallying to Tom Clarke as opposed to John Redmond.

However, the influence of the Irish Republican Brotherhood could not be measured in numerical terms only. IRB men had infiltrated the leadership of every Irish Ireland movement of consequence, including the Gaelic League, the Gaelic Athletic Association and many other bodies. It may or may not have been an IRB man who prompted the vice-president of the Gaelic League, Professor Eoin MacNeill, to write a momentous article in the Gaelic League's official organ, *Claidheamh* (*The Bright Sword*), on the heels of the Ulster Volunteers' gun-running. The article put forward the idea that if the Ulster Volunteer Force could arm and organise to defeat Home Rule, perhaps it was time for Nationalists to arm and organise themselves to prevent Home Rule being defeated by force. Shortly after the article appeared in October 1913, a meeting to which MacNeill was invited was held in Wynne's Hotel, Dublin, at the instigation of the IRB. As Irish parliamentary sentiment and pro-British fervour were so strong, the IRB men kept themselves in the background. Only people of impeccable constitutionalist credentials were elected to a committee that decided to hold a public meeting at the Rotunda in

Dublin on 25 November, 1913, with a view to founding a Nationalist Volunteer Movement. In his opening speech MacNeill was careful to state that the proposed new body meant no ill towards the UVF:[22]

> We do not contemplate any hostility to the Volunteer movement that has already been initiated in parts of Ulster. The strength of that movement consists in men whose kinsfolk were amongst the foremost and the most resolute in winning freedom for the United States of America…The more genuine and successful the local Volunteer movement in Ulster becomes, the more completely does it establish the principle that Irishmen have the right to decide and govern their own national affairs. We have nothing to fear from the existing Volunteers in Ulster nor they from us.

His fire was trained on the Conservatives. The Volunteers' manifesto stated that:

> …A plan has been deliberately adopted by one of the great English political parties, advocated by the leaders of that party and by its numerous organs in the Press, and brought systematically to bear on English public opinion, to make a display of military force and the menace of armed violence the determining factor in the future relations between this country and Great Britain.

The huge attendance at the meeting showed that Nationalists were prepared to resist that menace. Some 4000 men enrolled at the meeting. Amongst them was Eamon de Valera who would live to become the most

famous Irishman of the century. The identity of de Valera's
father is a matter of some controversy. What is certain is that
he was born out of wedlock to an Irish mother, Katherine
Coll, in a foundling home in New York on 14 October, 1882.
From infancy he was reared by the Coll family at Bruree,
County Limerick. He was educated at the local National
School, then the Christian Brothers' School at Charleville
before progressing, via bursaries, to Blackrock College,
Dublin. He graduated from the Royal University (changed
by Birrell into the National University), eventually
becoming a mathematics teacher. Like many young men
of his time, he entered the national struggle through an
interest in the Irish language and membership of the Gaelic
League.

The new Volunteer force was constituted on democratic
lines. Any Volunteer, chosen without regard to class or
creed, could become a member of the Committee which
appointed officers. In parts of the country the Volunteers
selected their own officers. Col. Maurice Moore, a brother
of the novelist, George Moore, who was a Redmond
supporter and a member of the Connaught Rangers, one of
the most famous Irish regiments, was appointed Inspector
General of the new organisation. In a letter to Joe McGarrity
in America, Tom Clarke described the atmosphere
generated by the Rotunda meeting and what followed:[23]

> Joe, it is worth living in Ireland these times – there is an
> awakening – the slow, silent plodding, and the open preach-
> ing is at last showing results, things are in full swing on the
> upgrade – and we are breathing air that compels one to fling
> up his head and stand more erect.

...The volunteer movement caught on in great style here in Dublin. Such an outpouring of young fellows was never seen. They filled the Rink in the Rotunda Gardens (which holds 7000), filled the adjacent garden, overflowed into the large Concert Hall in the Rotunda buildings and packed the street around the entrances and afterwards 5000 people at least had tried to get up to entrance and had to go back home. The places were packed too closely to enable the stewards to move around inside and have enrolment forms filled, but even as it was there were about 4000 enrolled that night. – Then the drills – every drill hall packed since – too much packed to allow of satisfactory drilling – then the class of fellows who are there – and the enthusiasm and the National note in the atmosphere! – 'tis good to be in Ireland these times.

The government had taken alarm and issued a proclamation forbidding importation of arms. I hoped they wouldn't do so for some months, but the drilling will go ahead and already we know it is not going to cause any panicky feeling among the volunteers – hundreds of young fellows who could not be interested in the National Movement, even on the milk and water side are in these volunteers and are saying things which proves that the right spot has been touched in them by the volunteering. Wait till they get their fist clutching the steel barrel of a business rifle and then Irish instincts and Irish manhood can be relied upon...

As Clarke's letter indicates, the British Government had reacted to the Volunteers' formation by issuing a ban on the importation of arms, although no such ban had followed the formation of the UVF, another clear indication to

Nationalists that there was one law for them and another for the Ulster Volunteer Force. This belief was greatly strengthened the following April when the Orangemen openly landed their arms without a hand being raised to stop them. Drilling became widespread, with the Volunteers being trained both by ex-soldiers and by instructors who had gained their expertise as boys in the *Fianna*. Popular enthusiasm for the new force was such that as Clarke's letter indicates, recruits came in large numbers, not only from the Gaelic League and Sinn Fein but also from the ranks of supporters and followers of John Redmond. Their principal theoretician, Padraig Pearse, wrote:[24]

> Personally I think the Orangeman with the rifle a much less ridiculous figure than the Nationalist without a rifle...in the present circumstances accursed be the soul of any National-ist who would dream of firing a shot or draw on a sword against the Ulster Volunteers in connection with this bill. Any such action would be an enforcement of a British law on an Irish populous which refused it; would be a martialling under the Union Jack.

Just what Pearse thought the Ulster Volunteers intended to do with their rifles is a moot point. However, it became standard Republican dogma that somehow if Britain stood aside, the Orangemen would behave reasonably. The view permeated Provisional IRA thinking throughout the entire course of the contemporary 'Troubles'. However it was, and is, an attitude for which Pearse and those who thought, and think, like him were prepared to sacrifice their lives. As he stood in the dock, knowing that he was doomed, Roger

Casement declared before sentence of death was pronounced on him:[25]

> I know not how all my colleagues on the Volunteer commit-
> tee in Dublin reviewed the growing menace, but those with
> whom I was in closest co-operation redoubled, in face of
> these threats from without, our efforts to unite all Irishmen
> from within. Our appeals were made to Protestant and
> Unionist as much almost as to Catholic and Nationalist
> Irishmen. We hoped that by the exhibition of affection and
> goodwill on our part towards our political opponents in
> Ireland we would yet succeed in winning them from the side
> of an English Party…

Behind the noble aspirations of the Republicans, there lay the unpalatable and unacknowledged reality, that the outcome of Republicanism striving to be free and Orangeism seeking to maintain its supremacy, must inevitably be conflict. Carson, for one, had made it abundantly clear what he intended the Ulster Volunteer rifles to be used for: to prevent either their holders or himself having to live under a Dublin parliament. With the support of Bonar Law he had taken the question of Partition a step further soon after the UVF's formation. On 1 January, 1913 he had moved that the entire nine-county province of Ulster be excluded from the operation of the Home Rule Act. Redmond opposed this amendment as did Asquith and it was defeated. But Asquith bowed to the mounting threats of civil war by announcing that before the Home Rule Bill became law another election would have to be held.

Writing at this remove, it is difficult to grasp the extent to which the Conservative leadership was prepared to sail along the wilder shores of defiance to a point where the waters of politics broke over the reefs of treachery. Bonar Law, for example, in support of Carson's amendment, solemnly declared that the Ulster Unionists, rather than be ruled by the Nationalists would 'prefer to accept the Government of a foreign country'. This statement, made in London by the Leader of His Majesty's Loyal Opposition as the war clouds darkened over Europe, was clearly designed to be read in Berlin.

It was echoed by the man who actually sailed in the guns for the UVF, Major Fred Crawford, an officer in the British Army, who said that if Home Rule became effective he would: 'infinitely prefer to change his allegiance right over to the Emperor of Germany or anyone else who had got a proper and stable government'. Bonar Law also informed King George V that he would advise British Army officers to refuse any orders that directed them to take action against Ulster. Ironically, one of the few figures to stand out against such blackmail was Randolph Churchill's son, Winston. Far from proclaiming that Ulster would fight and Ulster would be right, he ordered a squadron to be held in readiness off the coast of Scotland, and so emphatically ruled that Ulster would not be right that he threatened that if Belfast showed fight, he would 'have the town in ruins in 24 hours'. An opportunity to test the Churchillian bellicosity never arose.

In an effort to resolve the Partition issue the king called a conference of all the interested parties at Buckingham Palace on 21 July, 1914. For four days, in Churchill's celebrated comment the conference 'toiled round the muddy by-ways of Fermanagh and Tyrone'. That is to say, the Irish and English leaders argued as to whether all nine counties of Ulster should be permanently excluded from the operation of the Home Rule Act or whether only the four with large Unionist populations should be partitioned. There was also a proposal before the meeting that 'county option' be exercised whereby any county by a vote of its internal majority could exclude itself from the operation of Home Rule for a period of six years.

Partition was thus firmly on the table. The reality of the situation at this stage was that far from being prepared to make any concessions to Nationalist sentiment, the UVF was on a war footing, only awaiting a telegram from Carson containing the words 'go ahead' to stage a *coup d'état* and set up a provisional government. Sir Henry Wilson had given his opinion that if the Army was told to intervene the result would be that: '...if Carson and his Government were sitting in the City Hall and we were ordered to close down the Hall, we would not go'. Not surprisingly the conference ended in failure, by coincidence, on the day the Austrian ultimatum was delivered to Serbia. Asquith was reporting the breakdown to the Cabinet on 24 July when the wording of the ultimatum was handed to Foreign Secretary Sir David Grey. In his book, *The World Crisis*, Churchill recorded the famous description of how as he heard Gray read aloud the fateful document: 'The parishes of Fermanagh and Tyrone faded back into the mists and squalls of Ireland, and a strange light began immediately, but by perceptible gradations, to fall and grow upon the map of Europe'.

Back in Ireland, as the last act of the parliamentary Home Rule drama played out at Westminster, Redmond had forced a measure of control on the newly formed Irish

Volunteers, which he correctly foresaw would pose a major threat to his position. After abortive private negotiations between his nominees and the Volunteers' leaders, Redmond went public in the press on 9 June, 1914, attacking the Volunteers' Committee as being 'non-Representative' and demanding that the Committee should be 'strengthened' by the addition of twenty-five nominees of his own 'in sympathy' with the 'policy and aims' of the Irish Party. Rather than have a split, the Volunteers agreed to Redmond's terms.

However, a split was unavoidable. The dichotomy in philosophy between the Redmondites and the physical force men was moving to its inevitable conclusion. On Sunday, 26 July, 1914, two days after the Buckingham Palace negotiation broke down, the yacht *Asgard*[26] and Erskine Childers sailed into history. The yacht, a wedding present for Childers, had been designed and built in Norway in 1905, ironically the year in which Norwegian independence was achieved – peacefully. *Asgard* is the Norwegian word for Home of the Gods.

Robert Erskine Childers was the orphan son of noted English oriental scholar, Robert Caesar Childers. He was raised by his mother's family, the Bartons, in Annamoe, County Wicklow. After graduating from Cambridge, he became a clerk in the House of Commons. His sailing experience provided the background for his famous novel, *The Riddle of the Sands*. This was such an authentic picture of a fictional plot by the Kaiser to invade England across the North Sea that the book is credited with causing the Royal Navy North Sea fleet to be expanded prior to World War I. Childers, who ultimately died before an Irish firing squad in the Irish Civil War, apparently started to become disenchanted with the White Anglo-Saxon Protestant civilising mission during the Boer War. He and his wife Mary 'Molly' Osgood of Boston were devout Home Rulers and in the wake of the Larne gun-running, it was to Childers and another Irish yachtsman, Conor O'Brien, that Mary Spring-Rice, a daughter of Lord Mounteagle, turned with a suggestion that arms purchased in Germany might be sailed into Dublin. Other prominent figures of the period who helped to raise and to donate money for the project were the historian Alice Stopford Green, the humanitarian Roger Casement and the novelist Darrel Figgis.

Childers and his wife sailed 900 rifles aboard the *Asgard* from a rendezvous point off the Ruytigen Lightship on the Belgian coast to Howth Harbour in County Dublin. Appropriately enough, they set off on the Orangemen's feast day, 12 July, 1914 and landed in broad daylight on a Sunday afternoon. Childers' 900 rifles were followed a few days later (Saturday, 1 August) by a consignment of 600 guns which were sailed to the Welsh coast aboard Conor O'Brien's *Kelpie*. Here they were trans-shipped to the yacht *Chotah*, owned by a Dublin surgeon, Sir Thomas Myles, and landed at Kilcoole on the Wicklow coast.

In the wake of the Howth landing, an event occurred which had a marked effect on Irish public opinion. Some 800 Volunteers had marched to Howth from Dublin seven miles away to meet the *Asgard*. On the way back to Dublin with the rifles, the Volunteers were halted by Assistant Commissioner Harrell of the Dublin Metropolitan Police, backed up by a company of the King's Own Scottish Borderers. Harrell demanded the rifles, was refused and ordered his police to disarm the Volunteers. A fist fight broke out in which a handful of participants on either side were injured and approximately a dozen rifles captured.

A number of the Volunteers who had only joined since Redmond had enforced his will on the organisation, had little or no training. Some of these broke ranks and fled, throwing away their weapons. Harrell then ended the confusion by calling off his men and staging fresh negotiations. During this parley, the Volunteers at the rear of the procession broke away and made off safely with their rifles, leaving Harrell virtually empty-handed. But then tragedy struck from another quarter. As the Borderers returned to their barracks, a hostile crowd gathered at Bachelors Walk and stoned the soldiers. The officer in charge, Major Haig, ordered his men to prepare to fire, but this was translated as an order to fire and a volley poured into the crowd, killing four people and wounding thirty-seven.

The behaviour of the Borderers towards the Dublin mob contrasted so sharply with the attitude of the British Army towards the Ulster Volunteers' arms landing that even the mildest of Nationalists saw the Bachelors Walk deaths as being the most stark indication yet of there being one law for the Green and another for the Orange. The IRB was secretly delighted at the hornets' nest of outrage which the shootings provoked. But the storm of indignation had only a week to rage before the outbreak of the Great War would overshadow everything.

Redmond rose in the House of Commons as soon as war was formally announced on 3 August by the Foreign Secretary, to state that the British Government might with confidence withdraw all their troops from Ireland, because the Irish Volunteers would cooperate with the Ulster Volunteers in protecting its shores. Carson had already pledged the UVF to the British for service either at home or abroad, and in light of the two pledges Lord Grey declared: 'The one bright spot in the very dreadful situation is Ireland. The position in Ireland – and this I should like to be clearly understood abroad – is not a consideration among the things we have to take into account now'. But Birrell, who liked and respected Redmond, judged afterwards, appropriately enough in the Irish leader's obituary in *The Times* that:[27] '...his famous speech in the House of Commons was a mistake, though a noble one. He took the curve too sharply and did not carry the train with him'.

In the wake of the Buckingham Palace conference the Home Rule Bill had indeed been placed on the statute book and given the royal assent, but at the same time (18 September) a Suspensory Act was passed postponing the operation of the Home Rule Act. Three days earlier, Asquith had told the House that the Home Rule Bill would:

> Not come into operation until Parliament should have the fullest opportunity, by an Amending Bill, of altering, modifying, or qualifying its provisions in such a way as to secure at any rate the general consent both of Ireland and the United Kingdom.

Where this 'consent' might be obtained, the Prime Minister did not say. Certainly it would not be forthcoming from the IRB who saw the war as an opportunity of following Wolfe Tone's dictum that 'England's difficulty is Ireland's opportunity'. There was also in the IRB a sense of moral obligation to fight that is difficult to understand today. Many of these men felt a sense of shame at being the first generation of Irishmen for 120 years not to have risen with arms in their hands. It was pointed out that they had missed the opportunity of a Rising during the Boer War, and that the chance provided by the Great War should not be passed up. But above all, their initiative in creating the Irish Volunteers had given them an army to rise with.

Accordingly, on or around 9 September, 1914, at a meeting in the office of Sean T. O'Kelly (who later became President of Ireland) in the Gaelic League building at 25 Parnell Square, Dublin, the Supreme Council of the Irish Republican Brotherhood called a small meeting at which it was decided that the war provided the opportunity for a Rising. Arthur Griffith was one of those present. So was Padraig Pearse who had been co-opted on to the Supreme Council the previous July. Writing about the meeting afterwards (in *An Phoblacht*, 30/4/16) O'Kelly said of Pearse, who was Director of Organisation in the Volunteers:[28]

> Padraig Pearse, probably the ablest and most inspiring figure of that time, interpreted worthily the traditional aspirations and ideals of Irish Nationalism, and symbolised in himself the unity of ideal of the different races that go to make the Irish Nation. He was well fitted to be chosen by his colleagues as the most outstanding figure of his time.

Padraig Henry Pearse, the son of an Irish mother and an English father, was born in Dublin in 1879 and educated at the Christian Brothers' School, Westland Row. He graduated at the Royal (later the National) University and became a barrister. He edited the official organ of the Gaelic League, *Claidheamh*, and was a prolific writer in both Irish and English and an advanced educational thinker. To further his ideal of a free and Gaelic Ireland, he founded and ran St Enda's, a school for boys at Cullenswood House, Dublin, and later transferred this to a larger setting at Rathfarnham at the foot of the Dublin mountains. By all accounts St Enda's was an excellent school, but was continually in debt, presumably contributed to by his preoccupation with matters revolutionary, which were so much a part of his daily life that a group of his pupils formed a Volunteer cadre and fought in 1916. Pearse was enrolled in the IRB during a visit to America. Subsequently his gifts as an orator and a writer led to his being appointed first President of the Irish Republic.

In the eyes of friend and foe alike he became the epitome of the ideal of the blood sacrifice, for two statements in particular which he made in 1915 as the storm clouds of 1916 gathered. The first was made in August at one of the great centrepiece rites of the Irish political and revolutionary traditions, the funeral, in this case the burial of O'Donovan Rossa, one of the heroes of Fenianism. Rossa had died in America but the IRB decided that he should be brought home to be buried. Because of his privations in English jails, the IRB ordered that during the trans-shipment of his coffin to a boat bound for Ireland after the Atlantic crossing the Volunteers should not allow his coffin to touch English soil. Standing at Rossa's graveside, 'in communion with that brave and splendid Gael', Pearse told a huge crowd at Glasnevin cemetery:

Life springs from death: and from the graves of patriotic men and women spring living nations. The Defenders of this Realm have worked well in secret and in the open. They think they have pacified Ireland. They think that they have purchased half of us and intimidated the other half. They think that they have foreseen everything; but the fools, the fools, the fools, the fools! – they have left us our Fenian dead, and while Ireland holds these graves, Ireland unfree shall never beat peace.

In December he wrote of the war:

The last sixteen months have been the most glorious in the history of Europe. Heroism has come back to the earth... the people themselves have gone into battle because to each the old voice that speaks out of the soil of a nation has spoken anew...Belgium defending her soil is heroic, and so is Turkey fighting with her back to Constantinople...The old heart of the earth needed to be warmed with the red wine of the battlefields. Such august homage was never before offered to God as this, the homage of millions of lives given gladly for love of country...war is a terrible thing and this is the most terrible of wars, but this war is not more terrible than the evils which it will end or help to end.

In the Ireland, indeed the Europe of the time, before the reality of the carnage on the battlefields sank in, such Rupert Brooke-like ideas were quite acceptable and touched a chord which would not be sounded today. But they do not represent the thinking of a man stirred to blood lust by war, rather the continuation of a train of thought Pearse had been developing for some years. As far back as 1897 he had said:

> The Gael is not like other men, the spade and the loom and the sword are not for him. But a destiny more glorious than that of Rome, more glorious than that of a Britain, awaits him to become the saviour of idealism in modern intellectual life, the regeneration and rejuvenation of the literature of the world, the instruction of the nations, the preaching of the gospel of nature and worship, hero-worship, God Worship – such is the destiny of the Gael.

To such a man, the notion of a Rising was an idea whose hour had struck. To his peers, and indeed given the Irish literary and missionary traditions, to successive generations, Pearse seemed both the embodiment and the exponent of Celtic idealism. He himself was the gentlest of men. Joseph McGrath, the founder of the Irish Sweepstakes told me the following story involving Pearse and Connolly a few days before the Rising:[29]

> We had just come out of a meeting somewhere in Dolphin's Barn. It was a lovely evening and Pearse looked up at the mountains and said: 'If necessary we can fight on in the mountains...' but Connolly interrupted him. He was a tough, rough man, a trade unionist, and he said in that northern accent of his: 'You'll fight in Dublin, Pearse'. Pearse stopped talking. He got red in the face, embarrassed. He was a nice fellow, very soft.

The IRB set up a military council to get control of the Volunteers and to plan the proposed insurrection. The IRB had officers throughout the Volunteers and it was arranged that when the decision to rise was put into operation, these men would take their orders from MacDermott and Pearse, not MacNeill. The Military Council consisted of Pearse, Clarke, MacDermott and Plunkett. Later they would form themselves into a Provisional Revolutionary Government with the addition of three other names – James Connolly, who took charge of the military operations during the Rising, Eamonn Kent and Thomas MacDonagh.

Eamonn Kent (Irish form, Ceannt) was born in County Galway in 1881. He played the Uilean Pipes, the Irish version of the bagpipes and was a member of the governing council of the Gaelic League. Thomas MacDonagh was born at Cloughjordan in County Tipperary in 1878 and educated at Rockwell College, Cashel. A poet and critic, he was a lecturer in English at University College, Dublin, and taught under Pearse at St Enda's School. His cottage at the foot of the Dublin mountains was a centre of both literary and revolutionary thought. Curiously, for someone who spent his life in defence of both literary and political freedom of expression, and who, had he lived, would probably have become known as the best poet amongst the 1916 men, one of his heroes was the poet-hating, book-burning Florentine monk Savonarola. Some of MacDonagh's verse was prophetic to the point of being obituaristic:

> *His songs were a little phrase*
> *Of eternal song*
> *Drowned in the harping of lays*
> *More loud and long*

His deed was a single word
Called out alone
In a night where no echo stirred
To laughter or moan

But his song's new soul shall shrill
The loud harps dumb
And his deed the echoes fill
When the dawn is come.

Joseph Mary Plunkett, who drew up the military plans for the Rising, was one of the three sons of Count Plunkett who fought in the GPO; the other sons were George and Jack. Plunkett was born in Dublin in 1887 and in spite of continuous ill health, led an active life. He studied science and philosophy, wrote poetry, worked with Thomas MacDonagh and others in founding the Irish Theatre and edited the *Irish Review*. He was one of the founders of the Volunteers and was a member of their first Executive in 1913. Becoming a member of the IRB, he was sent on secret missions to the Continent and to America in 1915 in order to raise support for a Rising. An exotic, highly visible figure, given to wearing bangles, jewellery and flowing cloaks, paradoxically, he also had a taste for conspiracy and undercover work. He gave Michael Collins a copy of Chesterton's *The Man Who Was Thursday: a Nightmare* and advised him to act on the chief anarchist's advice: 'If you don't appear to be hiding, nobody seeks you out'. Collins subsequently acted on that advice with spectacular results. Plunkett was appointed Director of Military Operations in 1916.

Plunkett's plans for the Rising were like all Irish
Republican plotting, mindful of precedent from the past.
They were heavily influenced by those drawn up by Robert
Emmet for his doomed insurrection in 1803. In Dublin main
buildings were to be seized and the roads and railways
interdicted so that no military reinforcements could get into
the city. As a last resort, the Volunteers were to fall back
upon the GPO which was designated as the Rising's
headquarters, and then to retreat northwards to Tyrone, to
link up with Volunteer units from the north. The whole
thing was based on German arms arriving. The rebels even
looked forward to receiving assistance from a German
submarine in Dublin Bay. Artillery was also expected from
Germany and there appeared to be a possibility of officers
and soldiers arriving. The Volunteers themselves did not
have even one machine gun and Plunkett's plan depended
on the certainty of the Provisional Government's ten
thousand or so Irish Volunteers coming out. There was also
the hoped-for possibility that once hostilities commenced,
Redmond's much larger National Volunteers would join in,
bringing the strength of the insurgents up to one hundred
thousand men. In the event none of these hopes was to be
realised.

The Rising was scheduled to take place if the English
tried to enforce conscription, or if the Germans invaded
Ireland, or if the war appeared to be ending. At the
insurrection's commencement, there was to be a declaration
of war on England, accompanied by a demand that the
Provisional Government should be represented at the
inevitable Peace Conference following the cessation of
hostilities. Many members of the Volunteer Executive,

including Eoin MacNeill, were kept in ignorance of the IRB's decision. It was particularly shielded from Redmond's nominees, but the outbreak of war precipitated a split between these forces and those nominally led by Eoin MacNeill.

The organisation was riven on the question of support for the war. Despite Bachelors Walk, a majority was in favour of recruitment to the British Army. Traditionally, Catholic Ireland had greater links with Catholic France than with Lutheran Germany, and the destruction of Louvain with its Celtic manuscripts elicited sympathy in another small country for 'plucky little Belgium'. Given the long history of Irish recruitment to British regiments, Redmond's pledge that Ireland was so loyal that Britain could safely withdraw her troops also struck a chord. The press was overwhelmingly pro-British, the public wore Union Jack badges and young Irish men were told that it was their patriotic duty to fight for England. White feathers fluttered about those who did not. Redmond joined with Asquith in promoting recruitment. This was anathema to the MacNeill-led faction. Their view was articulated by Griffith in his paper, *Sinn Fein*:[30]

Ireland is not at war with Germany. She has no quarrel with any continental power. England is at war with Germany, and Mr Redmond has offered England the services of the National Volunteers to defend Ireland. What has Ireland to defend, and whom has she to defend it against? Has she a native Constitution or a National Government to defend? All know that she has not. All know that both were wrested from her by the power to whom Mr Redmond offers the services of National Ireland. All know that Mr Redmond has made his offer without receiving a quid pro quo. There is no European Power waging war against the people of Ireland. There are two European Powers at war with the people who dominate Ireland from Dublin Castle. The call to the Volunteers to 'defend Ireland' is a call to them to defend the bureaucracy entrenched in that edifice.

Our duty is in no doubt. We are Irish Nationalists, and the only duty we can have is to stand for Ireland's interests, irrespective of the interests of England, or Germany, or any other foreign country. This week the British Government has passed measures through all stages – first reading, second reading, committee, third reading, and report – in the House of Commons in the space of six hours. Let it withdraw the present abortive Home Rule Bill, and pass in the same space of time a full measure of Home Rule, and Irishmen will have some reason to mobilise for the defence of their institutions. At present, they have none. In the alternative, let a Provisional Government be set up in Dublin by Mr Redmond and Sir Edward Carson, and we shall give it allegiance. But the confidence trick has been too often played upon us to deceive us again.

If the Irish Volunteers are to defend Ireland they must defend it for Ireland, under Ireland's flag, and under Irish officers. Otherwise they will only help to perpetuate the enslavement of their country.

The dichotomy between the Griffith-Redmond positions almost precipitated a premature mini-1916 when it became known that Redmond and Asquith were to speak in Dublin at the Mansion House in favour of recruiting. A group of

Volunteers led by James Connolly, Sean MacDermott and Tom Clarke met in a hall at Rutland Square where a plot was hatched to prevent the meeting taking place by seizing the hall and holding it by force of arms, fighting to the death of the last Volunteer if necessary. This particular sacrifice was rendered unnecessary by the discovery that the Mansion House was already strongly guarded by armed troops. However, Redmond brought the dispute within the Volunteers to a head by making a recruiting speech at Woodenbridge, County Wicklow, on 20 September, in which he urged his listeners to join the war 'in defence of right, freedom and religion'. Afterwards the MacNeill wing of the Volunteers issued a statement saying:[31]

> Mr Redmond, addressing a body of Irish Volunteers on last Sunday, has now announced for the Irish Volunteers a policy and programme fundamentally at variance with their own published and accepted aims and pledges, but with which his nominees are, of course, identified. He has declared it to be the duty of the Irish Volunteers to take foreign service under a Government which is not Irish. He has made this announcement without consulting the Provisional Committee, the Volunteers themselves, or the people of Ireland to whose service alone they are devoted. Having thus disregarded the Irish Volunteers and their solemn engagement, Mr Redmond is no longer entitled, through his nominees, to any place in the administration and guidance of the Irish Volunteer organisation.

By far the larger portion of the paper strength of the 180,000-strong Volunteer force went with Redmond, styling themselves National Volunteers and leaving the Irish Volunteers with an estimated 12,000.

It should be noted here that descriptions of the Volunteers containing so many tens of thousands in this or that section can be misleading. Numbers tended to go up in moments of excitement, such as the initial formation in the Rotunda, a new recruiting campaign, or rumours that London was thinking of imposing conscription. But when things settled down, numbers fell off. However, there was a core which took the Volunteers seriously, drilled determinedly, turned up when called for, and made whatever sacrifices were necessary, including paying out of their own, generally very meagre, wages for their rifles. The men who would turn out on Easter Monday were the core of the corps. Men like the Northumberland Road defender, James Grace, whom we shall encounter later. He had been in Canada where he had joined a territorial regiment to learn how to handle a rifle and returned to Ireland early in 1916 when he got a letter telling him:[32] 'We are waiting for you'.

On 19 May, 1915, Asquith reorganised his government. He formed a coalition with the Conservatives. It included eight Unionists, amongst them Bonar Law who became Secretary of State for the Colonies; Sir Edward Carson was made Attorney-General with a seat in Cabinet and F. E. Smith was given the post of Solicitor-General. The seamless manner in which those who preached treason one year were rewarded with Cabinet posts the next, not only underscored the unscrupulous use which the Conservatives and Unionists had made of the Home Rule issue, it raised the question as to how much of their campaign and the support it elicited had been animated not so much by anti-Liberal as anti-Irish feeling.

But an attempt to more fully explore such psychological labyrinths, while fascinating, would take us too far from our story. What we can be certain of is that the pain and political destruction that Redmond was to endure because of his belief that to act as he did would induce England to keep faith with Home Rule after the War was badly repaid. His son was one of the many Nationalists who was refused a commission. His brother was killed in the War. Nationalists were not allowed to form their own regiments. Ulster Protestants were, in spite of the fact that they had lately being planning a *coup d'état*. Lord Kitchener, the Minister for War, so detested Irish Nationalists that at a public gathering he ordered the removal of a banner emblazoned with a harp by patriotic ladies, for a Nationalist regiment which never materialised, while one embroidered with the Red Hand of Ulster was honoured. Lloyd George later judged that 'this sinister order constituted the first word in a new chapter of Irish history'.[33] Kitchener's action was but one of many factors which now contributed to the swelling Republican theme.

Augustine Birrell later said of the Unionists' inclusion in Cabinet that it was 'impossible to describe or over-estimate the effect of this in Ireland. The steps seemed to make an end of Home Rule'.[34] Redmond was offered a place in the Cabinet, but in face of the growing threat to his position from the Nationalists, turned it down, stipulating instead that Birrell remain Chief Secretary. Birrell had long realised that by caving in to the Tories and the Ulster Rebels over the Curragh mutiny, the British were storing up trouble for themselves, writing: 'Politics often consist of balancing one set of grave evils against another set, and after consideration the Cabinet, with my concurrence, decided to leave it alone, although by doing nothing they almost negate their right to become a Government at all'. By 1915, his judgement of the Government's performance was even more gloomy. His job had become 'odious and hateful', and he felt that the conceding of Cabinet posts to Unionist extremists had sounded the deathknell of Home Rule. He feared that the introduction of conscription would precipitate 'shipwreck and disturbances on a big scale in Ireland'. 'Ireland', he said, 'is, I am sure, in a rotten state – ripe for a row, without leadership.'[35]

In trying to avoid that row Birrell faced an impossible task. He wanted recruitment to succeed, but after the leniency shown to the UVF he knew that the introduction of conscription would be disastrous. After all that had gone before, there was no question of cracking down on the Nationalists for their drilling, increasingly strident sedition and anti-recruitment activities. Yet the War Office, the military and rightists in Cabinet were pressing for both a crackdown on what they saw as the Sinn Fein 'hate' press and the introduction of conscription. Some 150,000 Irish troops joined up voluntarily, but this did not satisfy the military securocrats like Field Marshal Sir Henry Wilson. To their basic ideological approach that it was Ireland's duty to provide her patriotic percentage of cannon fodder was added the pressure for manpower caused by the appalling carnage in the trenches. By this stage (from the outbreak of war to 15 February, 1916) the House of Commons was informed that approximately 100,000 Irishmen had joined up voluntarily. This lower total may have been artificially deflated to highlight the figures given in reply to a question to Birrell from Sir J. Lonsdale concerning the scale of the prize sought by the securocrats, the pool of military-aged manpower still remaining:

Ulster	159,640
Leinster	167,492
Munster	133,237
Connaught	80,330

It was indeed a temptingly untapped source of cannon fodder. For a time, however, Birrell managed to steer a skilful course between the Scylla of coercion and the Charybdis of rebellion. Piaras Beaslai wrote of Birrell years after he had resigned in disgrace:[36]

> There exists a curious idea in England to this day that Mr Asquith and Mr Birrell were in some mysterious way responsible for the Insurrection of Easter Week. As one who was working tooth and nail to bring about an insurrection, I can testify that the biggest obstacle that we had to contend against was the cleverness of Mr Birrell's policy. The one thing that would have rallied support to our side was drastic coercion on the part of the English Government; but Mr Birrell cleverly contrived to appear as not interfering with us, while taking care that we were effectually silenced. The Editors of anti-English papers and pamphlets were not proceeded against; the papers were not officially suppressed; but, under the Defence of the Realm Act, the printers who produced them were liable to be closed down.

As a result of the Defence of the Realm Act, there sprang up
what became known as 'the mosquito press' – pamphlets by
Pearse and other Republican polemicists, a succession of
short-lived newspapers with names like *The Spark*, *Honesty*
and even *Scissors and Paste*, which consisted of an effort to
get around the Dublin Castle censorship by only printing
items which had already appeared in mainstream
publications. Both the IRB's paper *Irish Freedom* and
Griffith's *Sinn Fein* were closed down. Appropriately
enough, a weekly *Nationality* edited by Griffith managed to
survive until the eve of the Rising itself. This comparative
longevity and that of the Volunteers' newspaper *The Irish
Volunteer* owed itself to the Republicans' utilisation of the
Nationalist adage that the Orangemen were loyal 'not to the
Crown but the half Crown' – they got the seditious journals
printed by an Orange firm in Belfast.

The energy, the polemics and the excitation of
Nationalist fervour, coming on the heels of the sabotaging of
the Home Rule Bill, had their effect. While no section of the
public at large favoured insurrection, juries began
acquitting men charged with making anti-recruiting
speeches after Sean MacDermott was sentenced to six
months in prison for the offence. Even possession of
explosives was not deemed a crime, following a landmark
case in which, after convincing evidence of possession had
been produced, a school-teacher, Alex McCabe, was
acquitted. The authorities began resorting to deportation as
a weapon. However, senior IRB men like Denis
McCullough and Ernest Blythe elected to disregard the
deportation orders and were brought before magistrates
who only had the power to sentence them to six-month

terms, albeit with hard labour. The defendants reckoned that the publicity and the sympathy generated by that Irish clarion call 'release the prisoners' more than justified the hardship.

Beaslai was correct in his assessment of Birrell's policy. The papers from 1916 (available in the Irish National Archives) make it clear that the authorities had a fairly clear idea of who the disaffected were; a particular eye was kept on those with known Sinn Fein sympathies who worked in radio transmission or the postal services. The Lord Lieutenant, Lord Wimborne, appointed in 1915, constantly urged that stern action should be taken against the Volunteers. Formerly Sir Ivor Churchill Guest, he was a cousin of Winston Churchill's and like his great relative, fond of brandy. He had been elevated to the peerage in 1910 as part of the Liberal move to strengthen its representation in the House of Lords. Three incidents which occurred in the run-up to the actual Rising should have swung the authorities to Wimborne's side of the argument.

Firstly, St Patrick's Day (17 March) was celebrated by the Volunteers staging a takeover of Dublin. The entire centre of the city was cordoned off as MacNeill took the salute during an impressive march past. The mock attacks on strategic buildings which characterised this display became more realistic three weeks later. At Tullamore, County Offaly, the Volunteers demonstrated against an Irish Regiment leaving for France, drawing on themselves the wrath of local Loyalists who attacked the Sinn Fein hall the following night. They were driven off by gunfire and for a time police and Volunteers traded shots with each other.

The GOC of the Irish Command, Major-General L. B.

Friend, correctly divining that a new spirit of militarism had entered the Volunteers, directed that Liberty Hall be raided, but his initiative was countermanded by Birrell, who feared that it would spark off widespread disorder. British Intelligence captured a letter from a Sinn Feiner that talked about an early Rising. But Sir Matthew Nathan, the Under Secretary, wrote in its margin:[37] 'The outbreak in the Summer I look upon as vague talk'. To which Birrell added: 'The whole letter is rubbish!'

Only Wimborne, imbued with Churchillian pugnacity, sensed that real trouble was imminent and pressed for arrests. In addition to the foregoing and many other indications of disaffection, the Irish Executive by this time also had the copies of messages which the famous British spymaster, Admiral Hall had intercepted between the Fenians in New York and the Germans in Berlin. However, Hall was so keen to keep his sources of information secret that the rulers of Ireland did not realise that the movement of ships referred to was not from New York, but Germany.

Birrell and Nathan do not appear to have smelt a rat as late as 19 April, Spy Wednesday, when a document purporting to be signed by General Friend, allegedly copied from Castle files, was made public. It gave a detailed account of a planned swoop on Sinn Fein. The document was a forgery which was passed on to the *Dublin Evening Mail* in an effort to precipitate a crisis. The censor killed the story but the paper's editor gave it to an alderman who read it out at a meeting of Dublin Corporation. The forgery produced the reaction it was intended to, a widespread belief that the British Government did not intend to implement Home Rule when the war ended and intended to justify its perfidy by provoking an insurrection. Birrell and Nathan merely dismissed the letter as a forgery. Friend thought so little of it that he departed to London for the weekend and was out of the country when the Rising commenced. None of the three realised that their administration was not the forgery's intended target. This was MacNeill. All along he opposed violence unless it was first directed at the Volunteers or if an effort was made to prevent the introduction of Home Rule by force. But now he fell for the forgery, issuing a general order to the Volunteers to be in readiness to defend both themselves and their arms.

To the last, Birrell acted out of a combination of distrust for the approaches favoured by the military mind and an acute awareness of the propaganda value to would-be insurgents of a too heavy-handed approach on the part of the authorities. The Irish language, like the carrying of hurley sticks (popularly known as the Tipperary rifle) by Volunteers at public meetings, was regarded as a badge of sedition[38] by some. Lawrence Ginnell made skilful use of this fact to ridicule the application of the Defence of the Realm Act in the House of Commons when he raised the question of a man being described as a German spy by police. The gentleman in question turned out to be a Mr Claude Chavasse, BA, Christ Church, Oxford, who when stopped by police near an Irish College at Ballingeary, replied to them in Irish. A fracas ensued, in the course of which Chavasse was told by the police that an Englishman should not speak Irish. By way of illustrating that this proposition did not appear unreasonable in some quarters at least, Hansard notes that there was 'laughter in the house'. Not at the police, but Ginnell who, in the course of raising Chavasse's case, stated that 'Irish was an asset in the neighbourhood of an Irish College'. The laughter came when the Speaker interrupted him saying: 'that is a matter of argument'. The argument between the two concepts of nationality was about to enter a bloody phase.

The final rehearsals for the 1916 drama before the curtain eventually went up on Easter Monday was a combination of Murphy's Law and stark tragedy. The blundering and mishaps on the part of the three central actors, the Irish, the British and the Germans would have been funny had they not been so fateful.

Taking the Germans first, it would appear that the behaviour of the Carsonites and the Conservatives was a factor in the German decision to go to war.[39] The Germans rendered assistance to both Orange and Green factions in the hope of making trouble for the British and to a degree, the Americans. When the Ulster Volunteers' weapons were being loaded at Hamburg, simultaneous and far larger loadings were going on aboard the *Bavaria*, *Kronprinzessin Cecilie* and the *Ypiranga* destined for Mexico where the Germans were contesting American influence. The openly declared sentiments of Unionist figures like the UVF gunrunner Fred Crawford that they would prefer Kaiser rule to that of John Redmond prompted the Ulster Liberal Association to publish a pamphlet entitled *The Kaiser's Ulster Friends*. The threat of civil war posed 'the Kaiser's Ulster friends' and their Conservative allies also caused experienced foreign observers in Berlin and Vienna to speculate on England's being unable to take any active part if war should come.

Carson met the Kaiser at a luncheon party in Homburg

in 1913 at which he agreed with the Kaiser that his opposition to Home Rule was based on a refusal 'to be ruled by the priests'. A month later the German strategist, General von Bernhardt wrote an article in the *Berlin Post* under the heading 'Ireland, England and Germany'. In it he said:

> ...it is not without interest to know that if it ever comes to war with England, Germany will have allies in the enemy's camp, who in given circumstances are resolved to bargain, and at any rate will constitute a grave anxiety for England, and perhaps tie fast a proportion of the English troops.

The lunch with the Kaiser sparked rumours of German support for the Orangemen in Ulster to such an extent that *The Irish Churchman* declared, on 14 November:

> We have the offer of aid from a powerful continental monarch who, if Home Rule is forced on the Protestants of Ireland, is prepared to send an army sufficient to release England of any further trouble in Ireland by attaching it to his dominion... And should our King sign the Home Rule Bill, the Protestants of Ireland will welcome this continental deliverer as their forefathers under similar circumstances did once before.

It was later reported in 1917 to the House of Commons by John Dillon, the Irish Parliamentary Party leader, that Von Kuhlmann, the respected counsellor of the German Embassy in London had visited leading Unionists in Belfast incognito as close to the outbreak of war as 12 July, 1914. His report, said Dillon, made the Emperor 'determined to go on with the war'. Quoting a variety of sources, including Lord Riddell's *War Diary* and the *Daily Telegraph*, an historian of Republicanism, Dorothy Macardle notes that:

> It was the view of Mr Gerard, United States Ambassador in Berlin at that time, that the German Department of Foreign Affairs, and indeed all Berlin, believed that England was so occupied by rebellion in Ulster and agitation throughout Ireland that she would not declare war.

The Austrians also seem to have taken the possibility of 'allies in the enemy's camp' into consideration. The historian of unionism, A. T. Q. Stewart notes that:

> On 26 July Dr E J Dillon, a special correspondent in Vienna, telegraphed his newspaper that one of the reasons why Austria expected a free hand in dealing with Serbia was that the British Government was absorbed 'in forecasting and preparing for the fateful consequences of its internal policy in regard to Irish Home Rule, which may, it is apprehended, culminate in civil war'.

Whatever the weight of the Orange component of the Irish argument in the German decision to go to war may have been, once it was made the Green side immediately contacted the Germans through John Devoy in New York. Devoy and a delegation from *Clan na Gael* were met by the German Ambassador to America, Count von Bernstorff and his military attaché Captain Franz von Pappen. Devoy informed von Bernstorff that it had been decided to seize the opportunity presented by the war to stage a Rising with a view to ending British rule in Ireland and setting up an independent government. The Irishmen told the Germans that they wanted no money, what they sought were arms and trained officers which they lacked. As a result of the meeting Devoy subsequently sent an emissary, John Kenny, to Berlin with a document outlining the Clan's history and the revolutionaries' requirements. The Irish delegation felt that it had been well and sympathetically received but in fact, in reporting to Berlin, the Ambassador opposed the Irish request because he feared it would give American Anglophiles ammunition to use against Germany. The von Bernstorff approach of sympathy but little tangible assistance was to characterise German dealings with the IRB, as Roger Casement in particular was to discover for himself.

Casement was born in 1864, the son of Ulster Protestants of County Antrim. After entering the British Consular Service he did distinguished work in exposing the ill-treatment of native labourers in the Belgian Congo and in the Putumayo in Latin America. In recognition of this, he received a knighthood. He wrote poems, articles and diaries and subscribed money towards the restoration of the Irish language. His espousal of the Irish cause inspired the British to regard him with loathing, particularly after he went to Germany. Birrell customarily referred to him as 'the Lunatic'. Casement's habit of interpolating his diary with comments which indicated his homosexuality, helped to get him hanged. The British circulated copies of the diary particularly in Washington, where their contents diminished support for his reprieve. Birrell also induced John Redmond to be less ardent in Casement's defence by showing him the diaries.

Casement travelled from New York to Germany under an assumed name, having first shaved off his beard to disguise himself from the British agents who followed him everywhere. At Christina in Norway the British Consul made an unsuccessful attempt to have him murdered, but he reached Berlin safely on 31 October, 1914 and began a series of meetings at the Foreign Office. On 20 November the *Norddeutsche Allgemeine Zeitung* published an official statement of the German Imperial Government's friendly attitude towards the Irish people and wishes for their attainment of independence. On 27 December an undertaking was signed in Berlin between Casement as 'Irish Envoy' and the German State Secretary Von Simmerman, and stamped with the Seal of the German Chancellor.

By this it was agreed that an Irish Brigade should be formed from among the prisoners-of-war, and this brigade was to serve Ireland solely and not to be employed or directed to German ends. None but Irish officers were to conduct military operations of the brigade. It was to be furnished and equipped by the German Imperial Government as a free gift to aid the cause of Irish independence. No member was to receive any pay or money from the German Government: it was to be a Volunteer Brigade. In the event of a German naval victory, the German Government was to send the Irish Brigade to Ireland with an ample supply of arms and ammunition. If with the help of the Brigade the Irish people should succeed in establishing an independent Irish Government, the German Government was to give it public recognition, support and goodwill.

The Irish Brigade never materialised. With a handful of exceptions the Irish prisoners-of-war refused to join (back at home their relatives were still drawing their allowances) and Casement became increasingly disillusioned with his mission and the sincerity of his host's intentions towards Ireland. However, Joseph Plunkett, who also visited Berlin early in 1915, was promised a shipload of arms to be sent to Ireland the following spring. Plunkett and the Foreign Office official, Von Bethmann Holweig, agreed that an Irish insurrection timed to coincide with a German offensive on the Western Front would be of help to Germany. Plunkett and Casement were also led to believe that the original Devoy request for German officers, preferably accompanied by an expeditionary force armed with artillery, was a real possibility.

Back in Ireland the IRB now faced more problems than they had realised in their preparations for the promised spring Rising. The war had disrupted communications across the Atlantic. The IRB believed that it had circumvented this difficulty by using one Tommy O'Connor, a steward on an Atlantic liner, to carry messages between Dublin and Devoy. Using O'Connor would obviate the risk of telegraphic interception. In fact, interception had taken place – by British Naval Intelligence. Captain, later Admiral Sir Reginald Hall and his team in Room 40 at the Admiralty had cracked the German codes so that everything that passed between the German Embassy in Washington and the Foreign Office in Berlin was known to London. Putting together this information and various letters seized in the mail (and thoroughly studied before being passed on to their recipients) had alerted the Admiralty to the fact that something was likely to happen during Easter 1916.

But Murphy's Law also affected the British. The Dublin Executive took no action despite being informed that a ship had left for Germany to arrive in Ireland on 21 April where 'a Rising had been planned for Easter Eve'. Lack of liaison between the naval and military authorities meant that the message was not properly assessed – Lord Wimborne apparently thought that the ship was coming from America. The ship was the *Libau*, renamed the *Aud*, an allegedly neutral Norwegian vessel which sailed from Lubeck under the command of Lieutenant Karl Spindler, on 9 April. Aboard were 20,000 rifles, a million rounds of ammunition and ten machine guns.

The original plan was for the arms to arrive off the Kerry coast at a time between nightfall on Holy Thursday and dawn on Easter Monday. But Murphy's Law set in. The conspirators decided that if the arms came in as early as Holy Thursday, the British would be alerted and could strike at them before the planned date of the Rising, Easter Sunday. Therefore it was decided to ask the Germans to delay the landings until after the Rising had begun.

Philomena Plunkett, a niece of Joseph Plunkett's, was sent to New York to explain the change in plan to John Devoy. However, she arrived almost a week after the arms ship had left from Germany. Devoy passed on the change of date, but the Germans decided that as the *Aud* had no wireless there was nothing to be done. Devoy's message to Dublin informing the revolutionaries of this, either did not get through or simply was not acted upon. In fact the Germans could have made contact with the *Aud*, because two days after it left Lubeck, Roger Casement also sailed for the *Aud*'s destination from Wilhelmshaven, aboard the submarine *U19*. It should have been possible to contact the submarine and have it notify the *Aud*.

Aboard the *U19*, under the command of Lieutenant Weisbach, the man who fired the torpedoes which sank the *Lusitania*, apart from Casement, were Daniel Bailey, one of the few Irish prisoners whom Casement had been able to recruit, and Robert Monteith, an officer in the Dublin Brigade of the Volunteers. By now Casement was neither a well nor a happy man. He was, in fact, returning to Ireland not with a view to taking part in a Rising but to calling it off. Casement had risen from a hospital bed in Munich in great anger and distress at the discovery that the Germans had no intention of sending either officers, an expeditionary force, or artillery to Ireland. His protests fell not only on unresponsive, but on contemptuous ears, his liaison officer with the Germans, Captain Nadolny, telling him bluntly that the Germans had little interest in Ireland beyond the hope of some military diversion and threatening him with the possibility of cancelling even the shipment of rifles. Ultimately, apart from sending the *Aud* and the *U19*, the most tangible evidence of German assistance would appear to have been a series of Zeppelin raids and a naval raid on the east coast of England during the first few days of the Rising. The raids, though they naturally created a certain amount of panic, were militarily insignificant.

But not merely does Murphy's Law stipulate that if things can go wrong, they will go wrong, its corollary is that when things go wrong, they can only get worse. Michael Collins was charged with the task of sending three radio experts to Kerry to destroy a government radio station at Valentia and to set up the Volunteers' own transmitter in some hiding place from which the Germans could be guided as they made landfall. But the car carrying the three took a wrong turning and drove off Ballykissane pier about two miles north of Killorglin, drowning all three. An even worse self-inflicted wound on the part of the insurgents was the failure to erect the two green lights at the designated landing place, which caused both arms ship and submarine to sail fruitlessly up and down Tralee Bay, waiting for a signal from the shore that never came.

In theory, neither vessel should have been able to reach the Irish coast because as a result of Admiral Hall's activities, the British Naval Command at Queenstown (now Cobh), County Cork, had instituted a high state of alert along the west coast of Ireland. Several ships were involved from St Patrick's Day onwards in searching the fjords and inlets of the coast and checking on the identity of approaching ships. These were augmented on Holy Thursday, the original date for the commencement of the arms landing period, by a cruiser and three destroyers. However, by a combination of skill and determination, Spindler won through to Tralee Bay. He first sailed so far north into the North Sea that by the time he turned for Ireland, he could well have been a genuine Norwegian. The *Aud* sailed past a couple of British warships before she reached Inishtooskert Island in Tralee Bay, the rendezvous point with the *U19*, on the afternoon of 20 April.

However, there was no sighting of the submarine. And Spindler sailed on into the bay, where after dark he began signalling Fenit Harbour in the unfulfilled hope of being shown the promised green lights. After hours of fruitless signalling, he anchored off Inishtooskert where he was accosted by a British vessel the following morning. Incredibly Spindler managed to bluff his way out of the danger by telling the vessel's captain that engine failure had forced him to anchor. A combination of forged papers and a sight of the pots and pans which were alleged to constitute the *Aud*'s cargo convinced the English captain of the truth of Spindler's story. He was not to be so lucky a second time. The Naval Authorities received a message that there was a suspicious vessel in Tralee Bay and sent an armed trawler, *Lord Heneage*, to investigate.

Seeing the boat bear down on him, Spindler hoisted his anchor and made full speed in a south-easterly direction. On the high seas, Spindler was intercepted by two British warships that initially let him pass but then orders were received from Queenstown that the *Aud* be brought into port. Spindler again tried to bluff his way past the vessels, maintaining that he couldn't understand the signals he was receiving until he was sent one that he could not pretend to misread – a shot across his bows. Spindler dutifully sailed for Queenstown but ordered his men into German Naval uniforms, transferred them into small boats and departed, leaving timed explosives to send the *Aud* to the bottom, taking with her what little prospect there had been of the Rising succeeding.

Meanwhile, the submarine commander, Lieutenant Weisbach, had also put in a stint uselessly searching for green lights. He had sighted Spindler quite close to him but for some reason made no effort to contact the *Aud*, and concentrated his efforts on locating the promised green lights which never materialised. The green lights had been furnished by Sean MacDermott to the Kerry Volunteers some weeks before the German vessels arrived, but were left hanging in the Volunteers Drill Hall in Tralee. Austin Stack, the Volunteer Commandant in the area, seems to have believed that the arms shipments were due to arrive some time between midday on Holy Saturday and the early hours of Easter Monday. He made no effort to hire a pilot until the day the *Aud* was actually sighted, Holy Thursday. On his return home from meeting Stack, the pilot actually saw the *Aud* lying in anchor, but as Stack had told him that the vessel would be a small one which would not arrive until Easter Sunday, he took no action. Neither did Stack, and the green lights remained hanging uselessly in the Drill Hall.

Finally, as Holy Thursday night wore on into Good Friday morning, Weisbach decided that he was risking his submarine unnecessarily by loitering in Tralee Bay and decided to put Casement and his companions ashore. At approximately 2.30 a.m. and a mile or so offshore the three men, none of them seamen, were put into a small collapsible boat to row into the darkness. A few hundred yards from shore the heavy surf that characterises Kerry beaches overturned the boat, and they were lucky to get ashore, albeit in an exhausted condition. For a time, Casement was immobilised by hypothermia and was chafed back to life by Monteith, who later said that it was the regret of his life in view of what was to befall Casement, that he had not left him to die at the water's edge.

For Murphy's Law rapidly took a cruel turn. The collapsible boat was discovered shortly before dawn, as was a dagger, a thousand rounds of ammunition and three loaded revolvers. The police were sent for and shortly after midday on Good Friday, Casement was discovered hiding in a ruin known as MacKenna's Fort. Casement attempted to pass himself off as Richard Morton, a Buckinghamshire author. However, his claim to have written *A Life of St Brendan, the Navigator*, who was said to have discovered America after sailing from Kerry in a currach, weighed less with the policeman than the fact that some coded documents were found on him. He was sent by train to Dublin on the first leg of a doomed journey that ended on the scaffold the following August.

While the *U19* cruised the darkened waters of Tralee Bay, in far away Dublin the nominal leader of the Volunteers, Chief of Staff Eoin MacNeill, was discovering that he too had been operating in a darkness of a different kind. Bulmer Hobson, then the Volunteer's Secretary, had been alerted by two leading officers, J. J. O'Connell and Eimer Duffy, who had learned that Volunteer units throughout the country had received orders to take part in a Rising timed for Easter Sunday. The thunderstruck Hobson got MacNeill out of bed to tell him the startling news. MacNeill changed out of his pyjamas and, driven by Hobson, headed for Pearse's home to tell him in sulphuric terms what he thought of (a) his deception and (b) his Rising. After an angry harangue, MacNeill summed up his message by saying:

There'll be no waste of lives for which I am directly responsible. I will not allow a half-armed force to be called out. I can
promise you this; I'll do everything I can to stop a Rising –
everything, that is, short of ringing up Dublin Castle.

However, later in the day MacNeill cooled somewhat. Pearse had rallied MacDermott and MacDonagh to his side and they called on MacNeill who received them but stipulated that he would talk only with MacDermott, saying that he would have nothing to do with Pearse any more. Knowing nothing of what had happened in Kerry, MacDermott attempted to be straightforward at last about the IRB's plans. He told MacNeill that an arms landing in Kerry was imminent and that MacNeill would have to change his stance. MacNeill, however, continued to state his opposition to a Rising and his intention to do everything he could to prevent one. MacDermott pointed out that the IRB was the real controller of the Volunteers and that they were in a position to stop him preventing the Rising. But MacDermott's main point was that the arms landing meant that hostilities now were inevitable and that the Rising would have to go ahead.

This final point swayed MacNeill. He knew that the long-threatened crackdown must come in the wake of the arms landing, and he replied 'Well, if we have to fight or be suppressed, then I suppose I'm ready to fight'.[40] While MacDermott brought the good news to the others, MacNeill dressed and then entered his drawing room to shake hands with Pearse and invite everyone to stay to breakfast. However, the breakfast *bonhomie* did not survive the day. The O'Rahilly (the 'The' stems from an old Gaelic designation, denoting the Chieftain of the Clan, and indicates that the wearer is the senior living member of the family) discovered that Bulmer Hobson had been kidnapped by the IRB. The Quaker Hobson still believed firmly in MacNeill's original reason for founding the

Volunteers: they were to be used only if an effort was made to prevent the introduction of Home Rule by force, not for staging an Uprising. The O'Rahilly burst in upon Pearse, waving a revolver and telling him that anyone who kidnapped him would have to be a 'quicker shot'. The encounter did not come to shooting, but it reached no peaceful conclusion either. The O'Rahilly, a successful Kerry businessman, vehemently argued that Pearse's arguments for a Rising were not those of a practical man, but a poet and an idealist. This, of course, is exactly what they were. Pearse was on record[41] as saying:

> The European war has brought about a crisis which may contain, as yet hidden within it, the moment for which the generations have been waiting. It remains to be seen whether, if that moment reveals itself, we shall have the sight to see and the courage to do; or whether it shall be written of this generation, alone of all the generations of Ireland, that it had none among it who dared to make the ultimate sacrifice.

Failing to move Pearse, O'Rahilly decided the following morning to attempt to talk MacNeill into averting the Rising. He found MacNeill an easier mark than Pearse. The morning papers had carried reports saying that a man had been captured in Kerry after landing from a German submarine. Casement was not named but clearly the portents for a successful German arms landing were bad. MacNeill began writing out a set of countermanding orders to be delivered to all Volunteer units throughout the country, cancelling any instructions they might have received for staging a rebellion. He was strengthened in his resolve in this course of action when, around teatime, O'Rahilly returned bringing with him two Volunteers who had just reached Dublin from Kerry. MacNeill learned for the first time of the sinking of the *Aud* and the capture of Casement.

Furious, he had O'Rahilly drive him to St Enda's for a final confrontation with Pearse, who told him: 'We have used your name and influence for all their worth – now we don't need you any more. It's no use you trying to stop us. Our plans are laid and they will be carried out.'

'So well laid', MacNeill retorted, 'that the police at Ardfert have already upset them'. He warned Pearse that he intended to forbid any mobilisation. Pearse retorted that the IRB faction at least would not obey him and MacNeill stalked angrily out of the house, telling Pearse where he could be contacted. MacNeill hoped until ten o'clock that evening that he would be so contacted and informed that the Rising was off. However, realising that he need expect no word from Pearse to the IRB, he gave The O'Rahilly the following countermanding order: 'Volunteers completely deceived. All orders for special action are hereby cancelled and on no account will action be taken.'

The O'Rahilly then set off in his car on an incredible drive through several counties, distributing the order which was also disseminated by other couriers using any means of transport available. Having dispatched his countermanding order, MacNeill then proceeded to drive the final nail into the coffin. He caused the following announcement to be published in the *Dublin Sunday Independent*:

Owing to the very critical position, all orders given to Irish
Volunteers for tomorrow, Easter Sunday, are hereby
rescinded and no parades, marches, or other movement of
Irish Volunteers will take place. Each individual Volunteer
will obey this order strictly in every particular.

Insofar as any hope of military success was concerned, the
projected Rising was now a dead letter. Its only hope for
success now lay in the possibility that it would ignite the
flame of Fenianism in that generation – after, in Pearse's
words, its leaders had made the 'ultimate sacrifice'. Even the
supremely defiant Connolly was taken aback by MacNeill's
order. His daughter Nora had been in Dungannon on Easter
Saturday and had seen at first hand the confusion which it
had created amongst a large party of Volunteers, several
hundred strong, who had gathered in the town expecting a
mobilisation the next day. She had roused her father from
his sleep to warn him of the damage and confusion which
had been created. But the imperturbable Connolly had
reassured her: 'Pray God Nora, if there's no Rising, may an
earthquake swallow up Ireland', and then went back to bed.
But when he and the other members of the Provisional
Government who had met in Liberty Hall on Sunday
morning were handed a copy of MacNeill's *Sunday
Independent* and saw the wording in cold print, it was a
different matter; even Connolly was shaken.

Wearily the conspirators wrestled with the problem
MacNeill had posed them. Clarke felt they should go ahead
as planned, reckoning that once fighting broke out in
Dublin, Volunteers from all around the country would join
in. Pearse and MacDermott disagreed. The disagreement

centred not on the issue of calling off the Rising, but on whether to postpone or not to postpone. No one voted to give up. Finally, Connolly gave his casting vote in favour of a noontide commencement of battle the next day, 24 April, Easter Monday. After the meeting, the depression level was such that Clarke, that flint-edged Fenian, told Piaras Beaslai: 'MacNeill has ruined everything – all our plans. I feel like going away to cry.'

Looking at the actual mobilisation the following morning outside Liberty Hall, Clarke would have been forgiven his tears. Rifles were in such short supply that they had been augmented by pikes, the fearsome hooked weapon set on a long pole which had been used by the insurgents of 1798. More fearsome, however, were the Howth rifles which Erskine Childers had sailed in. These antiquated weapons were enormously heavy and dated from an earlier war. They fired a single shot with horrific effect. In a letter to Joe McGarrity in which he described the inadequacies of the guns, 'much inferior to the British service rifles', Pearse said:[42] 'the ammunition landed is useless. It consists of explosive bullets, which are against the rules of civilised warfare, and which therefore we are not serving out to the men'.

However, some of them certainly appear to have been served out, perhaps because no other ammunition was available, because one of the reasons for the rebels' post-Rising unpopularity was the terrible wounds which the bullets inflicted – it was said that exit wounds were twice the size of a man's hand. The insurgents also had some Lee Enfield rifles obtained from that never-failing source of Irish Republican armament, the British Tommy, a few Italian

Martinis and several shotguns. Some carried pick-axes, crowbars and sledge-hammers. Not surprisingly, Connolly whispered to William O'Brien, who was to succeed him as leader of the Irish Transport and General Workers' Union: 'Bill, we're going out to be slaughtered'. The only false prophecy that Connolly made that week was that the British, being capitalists, would not use artillery, because this would involve the destruction of property. In every other respect he was absolutely clear eyed; even to the extent of giving the last briefing to his men shortly before the Rising in which he said:

> The odds against us are a thousand to one. But if we should win, hold on to your rifles, because the Volunteers may have a different goal. Remember, we are not out only for political liberty, but for economic liberty as well. So hold on to your rifles!

Amongst those who moved off from Liberty Hall was Connolly's own son, Rory, who was fifteen years of age, and several others not yet twenty, including nineteen-year-old James Fox. Just before the mustering troops marched off to take their allotted vantage points, his father, leading the boy by the hand, had turned up saying:[43] 'Here's my lad – will you take him with you? I'm too old for the job myself'. A few days later, young Fox, hysterical and trying to flee the monstrous ordeal he found himself in, was cut to pieces by machine-gun fire as he attempted to climb the railings of the ill-chosen rebel strongpoint of St Stephen's Green.

Another doomed, last-minute arrival at Liberty Hall was The O'Rahilly. Having spent most of the night driving

through the country in an attempt to call off the Rising, he
now threw in his lot with the insurgents, saying: 'Well, I've
helped to wind up the clock – I might as well hear it strike!'
As it was well known that he was opposed to a Rising
(although not that he'd been attempting to call it off), his
gallant late arrival had a morale-boosting effect on men who
were going into battle literally, in one case at least, led by a
dying man, Joseph Plunkett.[44] Plunkett had had an
operation for glandular tuberculosis a few weeks earlier and
had to be helped out of bed and dressed by his aide-de-
camp, Michael Collins, who stood behind him, one of the
few present to wear a Volunteers uniform. Instead of
concentrating on what lay ahead, many of the other
Volunteers gave Collins 'a slagging' over his resplendent
appearance. At twelve o'clock Plunkett, Pearse and
Connolly led their rag, tag and bob-tail army up Abbey
Street, across O'Connell Street, into the General Post Office
and history.

Behind them followed their handful of men, O'Rahilly's
motorcar, now filled with guns and bombs, a number of
horse-drawn drays, a hansom cab and two motorbikes. Left
behind also, disconsolate at Liberty Hall, was one of
Pearse's sisters, who at the last moment as the men formed
up, had fruitlessly pleaded with Pearse: 'Come home, Pat,
and leave all this foolishness!'

The rebels met no resistance. The Post Office was filled
with bank holiday crowds buying stamps, posting letters
and making phone calls. A few soldiers and policemen who
were in the building on such errands themselves were
immediately taken prisoner. The official armed guard of the
nerve centre of communications in Ireland turned out to be

a sergeant and six men – with no ammunition for their rifles. The sergeant, who was wounded before the absence of ammunition was discovered, was ordered to hospital in the custody of two Volunteers, arguing vehemently that he was on guard until six o'clock that evening and wouldn't leave his post until he was relieved.

Outside onlookers gathered in amazement as word spread that something out of order was happening. Their amazement would probably have been heightened had they been able to witness Michael Collins' first action. He poured two tierces of porter down the canteen drain, exclaiming:[45] 'They said we were drunk in '98. They won't be able to say it now'. Later in his career Collins would become a legend because of his myriad escapes from capture and death. It is a reasonable speculation that in none of these was he closer to extermination than at that moment. But his behaviour foreshadowed that of the Volunteers throughout the fighting. Drink was eschewed, even when a public house was commandeered. The rebels took every precaution they could to protect the valuables of those whose homes they took over. When they did so one of their mantras was: 'After the revolution you will be fully paid back by the Government of the Irish Republic'. In banking terms this had all the weight of Confederate money, but in propaganda terms its value was immense for the insurgents' subsequent reputation.

One of the few deliberate destructions of property that occurred during the week brought a measure of popularity in its wake. It was caused by a James Joyce who worked seven days a week in a cellar as a bottle-washer for a notoriously bad employer, the owner of Davy's strategically located pub at Portobello Bridge. Given the joyful duty of seizing the pub Joyce burst in, rifle at the ready, to be greeted by Davy telling him that he was giving him a week's notice. Joyce replied:[46] 'I'm giving you five minutes' and opened fire on the bottles over Davy's head. Davy and his customers left the pub, rapidly.

More broken glass fell from the windows of the General Post Office as the rebels began using the furnishings to make barricades. Pearse appeared outside the GPO and proceeded to read to the onlookers the Proclamation of the Easter Rising,[47] the root text of the situation (*see the picture section for a facsimile of the Proclamation*).

After Pearse had finished reading, Connolly shook his hand saying: 'Thanks be to God, Pearse, that we lived to see this day!' Pearse's sparse audience was less impressed. After the reading a copy of the Proclamation was placed at the foot of Nelson's Pillar, weighted down by stones, so that passersby could read for themselves what was happening.

On the roof of the GPO itself, Gearoid O'Sullivan, the youngest Volunteer officer in the GPO, provided further clues. Instead of the normal Union Jacks which bore the Cross of St Patrick symbolising the Act of Union which the revolutionaries wished to destroy, he hoisted two other flags containing potent symbols. One was the traditional Irish flag, green with a golden harp but emblazoned with an unusual legend – Irish Republic. The other was the tricolour, the flag of today's Irish Republic. It was first given to the Young Irelanders instead of the hoped-for arms by Lamartine, the French politician and poet. Its hopeful but still unfulfilled message was green for the Gaelic tradition, orange for that of the Unionists and white for peace between them.

By appending their signatures to the dangerous political camping site near the stars which the Proclamation represented, Pearse and his comrades forfeited their lives on behalf of their fellow citizens. It would be pleasant to record that the gesture was appreciated. But on 24 April, 1916, Lilliput ruled Dublin. Both Proclamation and Flag were greeted with a combination of apathy and cynicism. The streets were filled with gawkers and would-be looters according to L. G. Redmond-Howard, a nephew of John Redmond, who watched the proceedings from the balcony of the Metropole Hotel:[48] 'There was practically no response whatever from the people; it seemed the very antithesis of the emancipation of the race, as we see it, say, in the capture of the Bastille in the French Revolution'. Redmond-Howard described how the crowd reacted when a boy with copies of the Proclamation emerged from the GPO:

> Instead of eagerly scanning the sheets and picking out the watchwords of the new liberty, or glowing with enthusiastic admiration at the phrases or sentiments, most of the crowd 'bought a couple as souvenirs' – some with the cute business instinct 'that they'd be worth a fiver each some day, when the beggars were hanged'.

Later in the week, one Volunteer officer in the GPO who had fought with the Boers described the locating of the general headquarters in the General Post Office as a 'mad business'. He, like many others, in particular Michael Collins who as a result transformed the rules governing Anglo-Irish warfare from 'static warfare' into guerrilla activities, saw the folly of the rebels cooping themselves up in one building with flags over their heads to indicate where artillery fire could most advantageously be directed. But the lack of military expertise was not confined to the Irish alone. Incredibly, the first response on that Easter Monday to the Dubliners' oft-asked question 'what is the military going to do about this?', came in the late afternoon from a troop of Lancers under the command of one Colonel Hammond. The good Colonel ordered a cavalry charge down the middle of Sackville Street. Had the rebels been more experienced the troop would have been wiped out, but as it was many rebels disregarded Connolly's instructions to let the horsemen get within killing range before opening fire. As a result, only a handful of soldiers were killed, but it gave first blood to the rebels who for some time were in more danger from their own continuously accidentally discharged weapons than they were from the British. But only initially, for more serious testing of the insurgents' mettle was to come shortly.

Brigadier-General W. H. M. Lowe, Commanding Officer of the Reserve Cavalry Brigade at the Curragh, had a total of 4650 men under his command at the Rising's commencement. Many of these were already deployed in barracks around the city, the rest were in the Curragh Camp in County Kildare from where they were dispatched to Dublin within hours of the Rising's commencement. An additional thousand were sent from Belfast. Within two days still further thousands of reinforcements set sail from England. The soldiers were supplemented by artillery and machine guns. With perhaps unconscious symbolism, the first British deployment of one of their 18-pound artillery pieces was at Grangegorman Lunatic Asylum. Lowe put in motion a battle plan to drive a wedge between the principal rebel positions, a line of fortified strongpoints running from Kingsbridge (now Heuston Station), the major railway station for the south, to Dublin Castle and on to Trinity College. Another looped cordon enclosed the GPO and the Four Courts in order to cut off the insurgents' headquarters in the GPO from their outposts. By the end of the week these arrangements, equipment and overwhelmingly superior manpower would have crushed the rebellion.

The city's most immediate threats came not from the rebels or military but from the lack of food supplies, gas and – curiosity. The initial response of the Dublin crowds was to treat the Rising as a spectator sport, gathering at vantage points behind the cordons of military that slowly began to encircle the insurgents. As this book was being written, Mabel Fox, who lived in Rialto near the South Dublin Union (now St James's Hospital), told me her memory of being taken as a six-year-old by her father to see the soldiers firing on rebel-held positions in the Union. 'I remember peeping out from under his coat, holding his hand. The bullets were flying. It was very exciting.' For many a Dubliner it was fatally exciting. Stray bullets snuffed out lives indiscriminately. A three-year-old child here, a nun there, a priest hurrying to a sick call, men and women standing at doorways or sheltering in their bedrooms were amongst the innocent civilians who formed what the Americans now refer to as collateral damage.

One of the features of the Rising was the Dublin mob who, once incredulity at the fact of no police appearing had worn off, began looting and setting fire to premises close to the GPO. In his book, *On Another Man's Wound*, Ernie O'Malley gave a memorable description of the looters' activities:[49]

...shops had been looted: Lawrence's Toy Bazaar and some jewellers. Diamond rings and pocketfuls of gold watches were selling for sixpence and a shilling, and one was cursed if one did not buy. Women and girls, some clad in Russian leather boots, smart tweed skirts and a shawl, wore rings on every finger, throbbing rows of them, only the joints showing. Ragged boys wearing old boots, brown and black, tramped up and down with air rifles on their shoulders or played cowboys and Indians, armed with black pistols supplied with long rows of paper caps. Little girls hugged teddy bears and dolls as if they could hardly believe their good fortune. Kiddies carried golf bags and acted as caddies to young gentlemen in bright football jerseys and tall hats, who hit golf balls with their clubs, or indeed anything that came in their way. This was a holiday. Some of the women with wispy, greasy hair and blousy figures, walked around in evening dress. Young girls wore long silk dresses. A saucy girl flipped a fan with a hand wristleted by a thick gold chain; she wore a sable fur coat, the pockets overhung with stockings and pale pink drawers; on her head was a wide black hat to which she had pinned streamers of blue silk ribbon. She strutted in larkish delight calling to others less splendid: 'How do yez like me now? Any chanst of yer washing, ma'am?' In the back streets men and women sprawled about, drunk, piles of empty and smashed bottles lying around.

As the GPO was being fortified, the rebels moved through the city in groups of twenty-five and thirty to take over strongpoints which, it was initially envisaged, would be held by forces with at least a couple of noughts at the end of each number. The South Dublin Union, Jameson's Distillery, Boland's Bakery and its attendant vantage points, Clanwilliam House and 25 Northumberland Road; Jacob's Biscuit Factory, the Four Courts and St Stephen's Green. The tiny amount of manpower available to the rebels was the main reason why Dublin Castle, the most important target of all, was not seized by them. A party of Citizen Army men burst in the main Castle gate, killing a policeman, frightening away the sentry and capturing the soldiers manning the guardroom.

The Castle thus lay at their mercy, but not knowing that most of the officers who might have led a resistance were gone to watch the Irish Grand National at Fairyhouse Racecourse, the rebels hesitated. The party that burst into the Castle was not reinforced and instead a number of other vantage points were seized, including a gents outfitters facing the Castle, the *Evening Mail* office and City Hall. This dispersal of effort allowed the British to reinforce the Castle a couple of hours after the attack began, and so the chance of seizing and perhaps destroying this symbol of British rule in Ireland was lost. The leader of the rebels, John Connolly, who was accompanied in the assault by his fourteen-year-old brother Matthew, was shot dead on the roof of City Hall two hours after the Castle attack began.

Confusion and lack of manpower further complicated the ruin of the IRB's plans. No effort was made to seize a number of strongpoints which would have been invaluable to the Volunteers, and whose loss proved correspondingly catastrophic. Trinity College, in the heart of Dublin, was not taken, nor was the Shelbourne Hotel, which overlooks St Stephen's Green. Both were seized by the British. As a result, rebels under the command of Countess Markievicz and Commandant Michael Mallin found themselves looking up into the mouths of blazing machine guns as they desperately clawed for shelter in tulip beds. The insurgents were soon driven out of the Green and forced to commandeer instead the College of Surgeons where their subsequent sturdy defence indicated what they could have done had the Shelbourne and not the flowerbeds been taken over. Possibly the most telling loss was the Crown Alley Telephone Exchange. A party of Volunteers was on its way to seize this vital communication link when a Dublin 'oul one' appeared, seemingly to shout a helpful warning to the rebels: 'Go back, boys, go back, the place is crammed with military'. Believing her, the rebels abandoned the effort to take the Exchange and five hours later it was taken over by the British military, having stood empty all day.

As teatime approached the British had begun to get a picture of what was happening and Baron Wimborne decided that it was time for him to get in on the Proclamation business which was to flourish throughout the week. He issued the following:

Whereas, an attempt, instigated and designed by the foreign enemies of our King and Country to incite rebellion in Ireland and thus endanger the safety of the United Kingdom, has been made by a reckless, though small, body of men, who have been guilty of insurrectionary acts in the City of Dublin:

Now, we, Ivor Churchill, Baron Wimborne, Lord Lieu-

tenant-General and Governor-General of Ireland, do hereby
warn all His Majesty's subjects that the sternest measures are
being, and will be, taken for the prompt suppression of the
existing disturbances, and the restoration of order:

And we do hereby enjoin all loyal and law-abiding
citizens to abstain from any acts of conduct which might
interfere with the action of the Executive Government, and,
in particular, we warn all citizens of the danger of unnecessarily frequenting the streets or public places, and of
assembling in crowds:

Given under our seal, this 24th day of April, 1916.

History does not record any perceptible reaction from the
GPO garrison to this document. Although the GPO was the
headquarters of the Provisional Government, and became
both the heart and the symbol of the Rising, all of the points
seized saw fierce and bloody fighting. With one or two
notable and nasty exceptions on the British side (which will
be described later), there was neither cowardice nor
deliberate cruelty from either side, although obviously a
revolution staged in a crowded city was inevitably going to
claim the lives of the innocent.

One of the earliest fatalities of the rebellion was also one
of the saddest. The rebels attempted to blow up the high
explosives depot in the Magazine Fort in Phoenix Park
around midday as a signal that the Rising had begun. But
the charges had to be placed against the wall of an
ammunition store instead because the officer in charge had
taken the key of the explosives room with him to the races.
Mrs Isabel Playfair, the wife of the fort's commander who
was away at the Great War with an Irish regiment, and her

three children were given a few minutes to get clear while
the rebels laid their charges and retreated. As they did so,
they saw one of the Playfair children, a boy who had just
turned seventeen, running to raise the alarm. The lad was
banging frantically on a hall door when Volunteer Gary
Holohan caught up with him and shot him dead just as the
door opened.[50] As he did so, the authorities were alerted
anyhow because at that moment, 12.25 p.m., the gelignite
that the rebels had planted went off.

Here two other strange notifications of the rebellion
deserve to be mentioned. One was that given to the pope by
Count Plunkett.[51] In the months preceding the Rising, the
Plunketts' spacious home and gardens, Larkfield, in
Kimmage, County Dublin had been host to a number of
young men such as Michael Collins, who had returned to
Dublin from London and elsewhere, so that they could fight
for Ireland, not England. They passed their time in
Larkfield drilling and learning how to make bombs, some of
which went off accidentally from time to time, leaving those
concerned entitled to count themselves extremely lucky to
have survived long enough to get themselves killed in the
Rising. But along with playing host to such anarchic
activities, Pere Plunkett was also a Papal Count and he was
chosen to go to Rome to inform Pope Benedict of the
impending Rising, both as a matter of courtesy and to assure
the Pontiff that there was nothing communistic about the
proposed proceedings. The Count made it plain: 'that it
was the wish of the leaders of the movement to act entirely
with the goodwill (or approval) of the pope and gave
assurances that they would act as Catholics'. The pope was
also assured that he need not be 'shocked or alarmed'. This

was a 'purely national movement for independence, the same as every nation has a right to'.

The pope, however, was both shocked and alarmed and wanted to know 'was there no peaceful way out of it'. When he was told 'no', he urged Plunkett to inform the Archbishop of Dublin, Dr Walsh. When Plunkett got to the Archbishop's House in Drumcondra, County Dublin that fateful Easter Monday he found that the Archbishop was ill. He was in the act of informing the Archbishop's thunderstruck secretary, Father Curran, of what was afoot, when the priest's phone rang to tell him that the GPO had just been attacked.

Christ having been put in the picture, Caesar's turn now came. Casement's arrest had at long last persuaded the British to act. Not long before Father Curran's phone rang, another call had been placed, this time from Dublin Castle to the GPO, by the Under Secretary Sir Matthew Nathan. It was to Sir Hamilton Norway, the Secretary of the General Post Office, asking him to join Nathan and Major Ivor Price, the Military Intelligence Officer in the Castle, at once. Correctly surmising that the meeting was connected with a requirement to take over the telephone service for military use, Norway immediately vacated his office and headed for the Castle through Dublin's peaceful, sun-lit streets. Behind him, ten minutes later the rebels walked into his office in the GPO. In the Castle, Norway was sitting in Nathan's office drawing up the written order needed for the telephonic takeover when a volley of rifle fire signalled Connolly's attack. The correct time of the commencement of the Rising had at long last been made known to the authorities in Dublin Castle.

The fighting was largely confined to Dublin, although throughout the country a few isolated engagements also passed into legend. The Fingal area of North County Dublin was largely taken over by a highly mobile party of fifty Volunteers led by Thomas Ashe and Richard Mulcahy, the precursor of the IRA 'flying columns' of the Anglo-Irish. Ashe had a motorbike and the rest had bicycles. They captured Swords, Donabate and Garretstown, and took part in a fairly significant assault at Ashbourne, County Meath, on Friday, 28 April. Ashe and his men laid successful siege to the RIC barracks in Ashbourne, but as the Volunteers were taking possession of the barracks, RIC reinforcements arrived from Navan in County Meath. A five-and-a-half-hour battle ensued in which eleven members of the RIC were killed, amongst them County Inspector Alexander Gray, who during the Land War of the 1880s had been a particular hate figure in Ashe's home district, Corca Duibhne in West Kerry. Several of the RIC party were wounded. Two Volunteers were killed and five wounded. At the end of the week Ashe and his men were among the few units that could have fought on, but laid down their weapons with the rest when ordered to surrender by Pearse.

Another much-talked-about incident occurred at Castlelyons in County Cork where the three Kent brothers, David, Thomas and Richard barricaded themselves in their home against an assault by the RIC who came to arrest them. They drove off the police, killing a head constable and then withstood a siege by a party of soldiers, their mother loading and reloading their rifles for them. Only after Richard had been killed and David severely wounded did they surrender. But in Cork City itself the confusion and countermands caused the Volunteers to remain inactive. Similarly in Limerick City where the Plunkett plan had been relying on a particularly important strategic mobilisation. In Wexford a mobilisation did occur, but only on the Wednesday, resulting in the bloodless and short-lived occupation of the town of Enniscorthy. In Galway Liam Mellowes took to the hills in the classic fashion of Irish guerrillas though the centuries, but not surprisingly did not encounter any army or police in those regions and no hostilities ensued. In County Louth the rebels captured the three-man RIC barracks in Castlebellingham.

In Dublin, outside the GPO itself, the principal theatre of death was on a section of the main road between Dublin and Kingstown (now Dun Laoghaire) lying on either side of Mount Street Bridge, known on one side of the bridge as Northumberland Road and on the other as Lower Mount Street. Along this roadway a group of Volunteers under the command of Captain Michael Malone, made of the area what was described subsequently either as 'Dublin's Dardanelles' or an 'Irish Thermopylae'. Mount Street Bridge and its precincts were part of a wide area under Eamon de Valera's command and included Boland's Mill and Bakery, Westland Row Railway Station (now Pearse Station) and Beggars Bush Barracks.

The last three strongpoints saw little fighting, but along the Mount Street Bridge approaches, a handful of insurgents inflicted some half of all the casualties suffered by the British during that week. The battle site could legitimately be held up as a paradigm of all the slaughter and waste on the Western Front. It began when a tired, dusty corps of middle-aged men known as the Georgius Rex or 'Gorgeous Wrecks', as Dubliners referred to this unit of home-defence veterans, were unwittingly marched straight into fire from the Northumberland Road strongpoint at point-blank range. They had been on manoeuvres that Easter Monday morning using unloaded rifles and were marched the six miles or so from Kingstown by their officer, Major Harris of the Trinity College Officer Training Corps, as soon as news of the Rising reached them. Not knowing that they were unarmed, the Volunteers scythed them down. Later, in the same solicitous spirit with which they helped the owners of the commandeered house to put away all their valuables so that nothing would be damaged or stolen during the fighting, the Volunteers' officers decided not to fire on men, even in khaki, who were not prepared for war.

But later in the week, when troops were landed at Kingstown, the Tommies were still unprepared. By then, especially after what had befallen the Georgius Rex, it should have been glaringly obvious that the posts were both dangerous and strongly held. Nevertheless the brass hats deliberately marched a squad of Sherwood Foresters, four deep, with no scouting parties, on to the rebels' killing ground. The first volley alone claimed ten young Tommies who, like the rest of their companions, were probably suffering from the effects of seasickness and a sleepless night spent crossing the Irish Sea.

Redmond-Howard has left an unforgettable description of the carnage which in the initial stages merited more the title of Dardanelles than that of Thermopylae:[52]

Along this road the troops had to pass, and they crouched down in long rows of heads – like great khaki caterpillars – in

a most terribly exposed order, so that if the rebel shot failed
to hit the first head it was bound to hit the second head, provided the rifle was anywhere in the vertical line. For the most
part the soldiers were boys in their early twenties, utterly
ignorant of the district, with orders to take the town which
was reported in the hands of a body of men whose very name
was a mysterious puzzle in communication, and not an
enemy in sight, only a mass of spectators up to within fifty
yards of them, and directly in front, blocking the street – the
rebel enemy meanwhile inside private houses to the right
and left of the narrow bridgehead they knew not where.

The first of their killers to turn up for revolutionary duties
the previous Easter Monday morning had been Volunteer
James Grace. Punctiliously, he arrived at the appointed
hour, eleven o'clock, and meeting point, the Catholic
University at Earlsforth Terrace, wearing his Volunteer
uniform and carrying his Lee Enfield rifle. Being a bank
holiday there were very few people about, and none of them
interested in revolution. Eventually, the man who was to be
the leading actor in the Mount Street drama arrived on his
bicycle. This was Captain Michael Malone, a likeable
personality and a good shot. Presently Grace and Malone
were joined by other Volunteers who stood around
unconcernedly like members of a team waiting for the
transport to take them to a football match.

By the time the company captain showed up, there were
thirty-four Volunteers in all, a fraction of what had been
expected; Company Captain Simon Donnelly had only
been promoted to that rank a little earlier by Eamon de
Valera because the original captain had refused to turn out.

Donnelly led twenty of the men to Boland's Mill approximately a mile away towards the sea where de Valera was headquartered. Malone and Grace, accompanied by two boys, Paddy Byrne and Michael Rowe, cycled to No. 25 Northumberland Road, which commanded not only the Kingstown Dublin Road, but a good view of Beggars Bush Barracks a couple of hundred yards to the east. Patrick Doyle and three men took over St Stephen's Parochial Hall, which overlooked both Mount Street Bridge and the Grand Canal, and across the road Denis O'Donoghue and a couple of men occupied the Parochial School. On the Dublin side of the Canal, to the left coming from the city, stood Clanwilliam House which dominated the surrounding streets. George Reynolds and the remaining four members of the party headed for this house.

'May we come in please?' enquired Reynolds. Once in, his first instruction was to warn his men to behave as 'representatives of the Irish Republic'. He ordered them to do as little damage as possible and to respect the inhabitants of the house. Later in the day, having fortified the premises as best he could, Reynolds suggested to one of the two ladies of the house that she gather up her valuables in a suitcase which could be locked away safely. The lady, a Miss Wilson, did as he suggested and Reynolds had one of his men carry the cases to a back bedroom, which was then locked and the key handed over to Miss Wilson. One of the rebels, a seventeen-year-old, had been unnerved by the Georgius Rex slaughter and sat shivering and sweating, incapable of action. He reacted with grateful alacrity when Reynolds suggested to him that he might like to go home for a spell and return later when he felt better. This left

Clanwilliam House defended by only four men. Meanwhile, a few hundred yards to the east, Eamon de Valera, at the command post for the Mount Street area, had more men at his disposal, some 120 in all. Unfortunately, he also had a far greater area to cover.

Plunkett's original plan had called for de Valera to occupy some sixteen posts in the area. These included a two-mile stretch of railway, a gas company, mills, a railway station and the bakery itself. Even if he had had the battalion at full strength, which the plan envisaged, it would have been an impossible task. However, de Valera made the best of a bad job, ordering his men to tunnel through cottages so that they commanded the entrance to Beggars Bush Barracks, from which it was imagined an onslaught would inevitably come. Barricades were erected at the nearby bridge over the Grand Canal by stripping bread vans of their wheels.

After a sleepless night, de Valera paraded his men and instructed everyone under the age of eighteen to go home. Those who went did so reluctantly, and two youngsters insisted on staying. One of them, Willie FitzGerald, was only fifteen, but though he was chased away repeatedly, he doggedly hung about until allowed to stay. In an effort to shift the other lad, Richard Perle, aged sixteen, his mother was sent for, but Richard despatched her with a lordly: 'Go home mother, this is no place for a woman'. Richard, at least, did not share James Connolly's views on the equality of women on the battlefield which had led to Countess Markievicz taking a commanding role in the fighting around St Stephen's Green.

De Valera also released from duty the bakery horses, which could not be fed. However, he rather vitiated the good opinion of Dubliners for this display of concern by cutting the gas company's pipe lines, thus ensuring that they too found it difficult to be fed. The difficulty was increased by the interruption to the bread supplies caused by his seizure of the huge bakery.

The assault on de Valera's men did not come until Wednesday morning. By then serious hostilities had taken place at various points in the city, at City Hall, St Stephen's Green, parts of Sackville Street and around the Mendicity Institute near the Four Courts. The Institute was defended by approximately twenty Volunteers under the command of twenty-five-year old Sean Heuston. Connolly had asked him to hold it for three or four hours to give the Four Courts garrison a chance to dig in. Heuston held it for fifty, against odds of twenty to one. His men made up for their lack of bombs by hurling the British hand grenades back at the soldiers – members of the Dublin Fusiliers. Four Volunteers died in the process but Heuston only gave up when his ammunition ran out.

The Four Courts, strategically located on the Quays commanding the southern entry to Dublin, was, with the ill-fated North King Street area, under the command of Ned Daly, Tom Clarke's brother-in-law. Yet despite the ferocity of the fighting, Daly, whose men had captured a large number of British officers and soldiers, insisted that the prisoners be given 'the best we had'. The South Dublin Union (now St James's Hospital) was an inappropriate place to seize, whatever arguments might be made about its strategic value, as inevitably fighting raged through wards filled with terrified patients who were housed in some of this vast sprawling complex of hospital buildings. Many of these patients were mentally ill. In attempting to protect them a Nurse Keogh was inadvertently shot by British troops. Nevertheless both sides showed extraordinary courage. An English officer, Captain Martyn, under heavy fire and cut off from his men but in possession of a box of hand grenades, single-handedly almost succeeded in breaching a key rebel strongpoint before finally being driven back when his bombs ran out.

On the Irish side Cathal Brugha passed into folklore as the contemporary embodiment of the legendary hero Cuchulain who tied himself to a tree stump during battle so that he should not fall from his wounds. Cuchulain's enemies only approached him when a raven perched on his shoulder, indicating that he was dead. Brugha, a Vice-Commandant whom a former colleague later described as being as brave and as stupid as a bull, received twenty-five wounds. He was defending a barricade erected to guard the Nurses' Home where the Volunteers' leader Eamonn Kent along with William Cosgrave, who later became an Irish Prime Minister, and a small group of rebels were located. He gave his watch to a subordinate to be given to his wife – if the Volunteer ever got out alive.

Then, his own life apparently forfeit, he turned to defend the barricade alone for as long as he could. Inside the Nurses' Home the Volunteers were dispirited and weary. It appeared that the end had come and while waiting for a final attack that they did not expect to survive, they joined Kent in saying a decade of the Rosary. Then from outside the Home they heard Brugha singing *God Save Ireland*. He had dragged himself to a position with his back to a wall where he could command the barricade and was challenging the

British to come over it. Reinvigorated, the rebels shook off their depression, remanned the barricade and kept the British at bay. Incredibly Brugha survived the Rising – to die six years later in a civil war at the hands of forces commanded by a government which included William Cosgrave.

By Wednesday morning the Mount Street units had not yet been tested under fire, although they were suffering from lack of food and sleep. However, their situation changed drastically following the arrival of strong forces of British troops at Kingstown Harbour throughout the night and early morning. Two columns of men set off for the Royal Hospital Kilmainham with instructions to clear all side streets and houses overlooking the two roads allocated to the columns; one, the upper route into Dublin via Donnybrook, the second, the lower route through Ballsbridge where the Royal Dublin Spring Show continued, seemingly in blissful ignorance of the waiting Volunteers 500 or 600 yards away. Incredibly, in view of what had befallen the Georgius Rex, the troops were equally ignorant. They were encouraged to remain so, despite the bloodthirsty rumours on which they had been fed since embarkation was ordered, by the fact that they were apparently welcome to the population at large. Fruit and food were pressed on them as they marched although some officers forbade them to eat it lest they be poisoned.

The deceptive friendliness was further heightened by a heart-warming little scene that occurred en route. One of the British officers, a Captain Dietrichsen, suddenly found himself hailed from a footpath by his two children. Because of the Zeppelin raids his wife had sent the children to

Dublin for safety. They were waving at the troops when they suddenly realised that their daddy was passing by. Dietrichsen dropped out of the marching column to hug his two children joyfully. A few hours later they were orphans. He was one of the first officers to die when the jaws of an ambush closed a few hundred yards away.

Had the soldiers swung left into Dublin along Pembroke Road a few hundred yards below Northumberland Road, they would have bypassed the men at de Valera's command completely and would not have encountered any opposition until they reached St Stephen's Green, where the Volunteers' position was vastly inferior to that taken up at Mount Street. But the young men in No. 25 were expecting the equally young and almost equally inexperienced soldiers. A few minutes before the Tommies appeared in the Volunteer sights, a sister of Jimmy Grace arrived with a despatch from Connolly, alerting Malone to the British landings at Kingstown and ordering that the utmost efforts must be made to stop them. Brigid Grace had also brought food for her brother and his friends but there was no way it could be passed through the barricaded door.

However, bullets could pass from behind the barricades. Such training as the troops had, and this generally consisted of some three months only, had prepared them for trench warfare. The idea of coming under fire in what could have been a well-to-do London suburb was utterly foreign to them. But they were ordered forward nonetheless. The Volunteers were astounded at the manner in which waves of soldiers, most of them obviously terrified, charged up the street. The Tommies were scythed down, Malone and Grace in particular creating terrible havoc. It took the

British a long time to work out where the fire was coming
from. Intelligence had warned them to expect trouble from
the school, but it was relatively late in the engagement before
the British discovered that Clanwilliam House was
occupied. Max Caulfield penned this moving account of
how the Tommies' attack looked to the rebels:[53]

For almost an hour there had not been a single movement
along the far side of the canal. The tree shadows had grown
perceptively on the still waters, broken now and then by a
slight ripple as the gentle breeze stroked it...Then the
defenders realised that the attack had begun again. In front
of them stretched an unforgettable sight. There were khaki
troops everywhere – crouched behind flights of front steps,
behind the garden hedges, behind the trees lining Northumberland Road. And lying in the road, especially lying in the
road. Four great khaki caterpillars pulsated towards them
like obscene monsters. Two lines had stretched themselves
in the gutters and two more crawled along on their bellies,
jammed against the coping stones. It was not like killing
men; it was more like trying to slaughter a great insect or
animal. Tom Walshe at once opened fire and just kept on
firing. As one man was killed, another crawled up and over
him. When he too reached the head of the line, he was either
killed or wounded. Sometimes as the caterpillar tried to
move forward – it could never advance beyond the group of
dead and wounded at the entrance to the bridge – it
appeared to be weaving from side to side as men elected to
move around a dead or wounded body rather than risk
crawling over it. Sometimes a few men at the head of the line
would rise up and attempt to charge the bridge, generally led

TOP The Citizen Army at Liberty Hall: The headquarters of the Irish Transport and General Workers Union bearing the banner 'We serve neither King nor Kaiser but Ireland!' Collection Sean O'Mahoney; ABOVE LEFT Constance Markievicz was a founder member of the Citizen Army and fought with the rebels at St Stephen's Green and the Royal College of Surgeons. She continued to take a prominent part in Irish politics until her death in 1927. National Museum of Ireland; ABOVE RIGHT Mary Spring-Rice and Mrs Childers photographed by Erskine Childers on his yacht, the Asgard, holding imported arms which were successfully landed at Howth Harbour. National Museum of Ireland

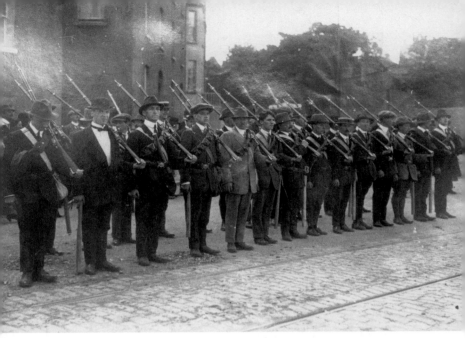

ABOVE Volunteers march to Howth to meet the Asgard and offload the rifles. National Museum of Ireland; BELOW Lord Wimbourne inspecting troops at Dublin Castle. He became Lord Lieutenant in 1915 and urged that stronger action be taken against the Volunteers in the period before the Rising. Cashman Collection

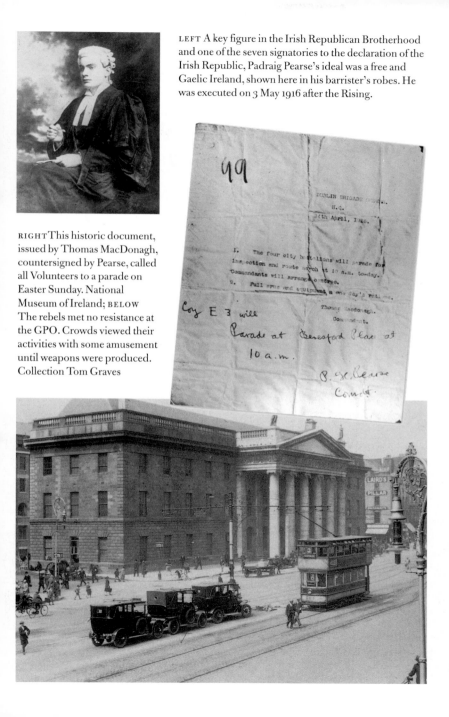

LEFT A key figure in the Irish Republican Brotherhood and one of the seven signatories to the declaration of the Irish Republic, Padraig Pearse's ideal was a free and Gaelic Ireland, shown here in his barrister's robes. He was executed on 3 May 1916 after the Rising.

RIGHT This historic document, issued by Thomas MacDonagh, countersigned by Pearse, called all Volunteers to a parade on Easter Sunday. National Museum of Ireland; BELOW The rebels met no resistance at the GPO. Crowds viewed their activities with some amusement until weapons were produced. Collection Tom Graves

LEFT Michael Collins was one of the few Volunteers dressed in full uniform during the Rising. Collins introduced the art of guerrilla warfare to Ireland and the world. Collection Tom Graves

RIGHT The Proclamation which Pearse read outside the GPO after the rebels had seized control. Collection Tom Graves

BELOW A British barricade on Talbot Street comes under fire from rebel positions. National Museum of Ireland

POBLACHT NA H EIREANN.

THE PROVISIONAL GOVERNMENT
OF THE

IRISH REPUBLIC

TO THE PEOPLE OF IRELAND.

IRISHMEN AND IRISHWOMEN: In the name of God and of the dead generations from which she receives her old tradition of nationhood, Ireland, through us, summons her children to her flag and strikes for her freedom.

Having organised and trained her manhood through her secret revolutionary organisation, the Irish Republican Brotherhood, and through her open military organisations, the Irish Volunteers and the Irish Citizen Army, having patiently perfected her discipline, having resolutely waited for the right moment to reveal itself, she now seizes that moment, and, supported by her exiled children in America and by gallant allies in Europe, but relying in the first on her own strength, she strikes in full confidence of victory.

We declare the right of the people of Ireland to the ownership of Ireland, and to the unfettered control of Irish destinies, to be sovereign and indefeasible. The long usurpation of that right by a foreign people and government has not extinguished the right, nor can it ever be extinguished except by the destruction of the Irish people. In every generation the Irish people have asserted their right to national freedom and sovereignty: six times during the past three hundred years they have asserted it in arms. Standing on that fundamental right and again asserting it in arms in the face of the world, we hereby proclaim the Irish Republic as a Sovereign Independent State, and we pledge our lives and the lives of our comrades-in-arms to the cause of its freedom, of its welfare, and of its exaltation among the nations.

The Irish Republic is entitled to, and hereby claims, the allegiance of every Irishman and Irishwoman. The Republic guarantees religious and civil liberty, equal rights and equal opportunities to all its citizens, and declares its resolve to pursue the happiness and prosperity of the whole nation and of all its parts, cherishing all the children of the nation equally, and oblivious of the differences carefully fostered by an alien government, which have divided a minority from the majority in the past.

Until our arms have brought the opportune moment for the establishment of a permanent National Government, representative of the whole people of Ireland and elected by the suffrages of all her men and women, the Provisional Government, hereby constituted, will administer the civil and military affairs of the Republic in trust for the people.

We place the cause of the Irish Republic under the protection of the Most High God, Whose blessing we invoke upon our arms, and we pray that no one who serves that cause will dishonour it by cowardice, inhumanity, or rapine. In this supreme hour the Irish nation must, by its valour and discipline and by the readiness of its children to sacrifice themselves for the common good, prove itself worthy of the august destiny to which it is called.

Signed on Behalf of the Provisional Government,

THOMAS J. CLARKE.
SEAN Mac DIARMADA.   THOMAS MacDONAGH.
P. H. PEARSE.   EAMONN CEANNT,
JAMES CONNOLLY.   JOSEPH PLUNKETT.

Reduced Facsimile of the Proclamation of the "Irish Republic"

Promulgated on Easter Sunday, 23rd April, 1916, at Liberty Hall, Dublin.
The seven signatories to this document were all executed.

A surrender note signed by
Pearse, James Connolly and
Thomas MacDonagh.
National Museum of Ireland

In order to prevent the further slaughter of Dublin
citizens, and in the hope of saving the lives of our
followers now surrounded and hopelessly outnumbered, the
members of the Provisional Government present at Head-
Quarters have agreed to an unconditional surrender, and the
Commandants of the various districts in the City and Country
will order their commands to lay down arms.

P. H. Pearse
29th April 1916
3.45 p.m.

I agree to these conditions for the men only
under my own Command in the Moore
Street District and for the men in
the Stephen's Green Command.

James Connolly
April 29/16

On consultation with Commandant Ceannt
and other officers I have decided to
agree to unconditional surrender also.

Thomas MacDonagh.

De Valera's surrender: he
was the only key figure of the
Rising not to be executed.
Collection Sean O'Mahoney

The leaders of the Rising were executed, mostly by firing squad in Dublin. Pictured are all those who were executed (from left to right): P.H. Pearse, Thomas Clarke, Thomas MacDonagh, Joseph Plunkett, Edward Daly, William Pearse, Michael O'Hanrahan, John MacBride, Eamonn Kent, Michael Mallin, Con Colbert, Sean Heuston, Sean MacDermott, James Connolly, Thomas Kent and Roger Casement. Collection Sean O'Mahoney

OPPOSITE PAGE:
ABOVE The heavy damage sustained by the GPO which was the first building seized by the rebels; they replaced the Union Jack with a green and gold Irish Republican flag which flew over the building throughout the conflict. National Museum of Ireland

BELOW The Aftermath: in Dublin more than 32 buildings and over 62 businesses were destroyed. Collection Sean O'Mahoney

ABOVE AND BELOW Booklets were published after the Rising, detailing the key events and characters, and also recording the damage inflicted on the city. Collection Sean O'Mahoney

by an officer with drawn revolver. None ever got beyond the half-way mark.

The killing could have been worse were it not for a combination of circumstances – the chivalry of the rebels, their paucity in numbers and their lack of experience. Tom Walshe of the Clanwilliam House Garrison knocked himself unconscious from the recoil of his rifle when he fired it at a running soldier. It was the first time he had pulled the trigger. Another factor which kept down the casualties was the heroism of the doctors, nurses and clergy from nearby Sir Patrick Dunn's Hospital who donned white coats and marched into the firing to attend to the wounded. The rebels allowed them to do so even though the soldiers understandably used the lull in the firing to attempt to find hiding places.

But more important than all the foregoing is the fact that while the killing could have been far worse, it could also have been far less had General Lowe not personally ordered his troops to the slaughter. The defenders of the tiny garrisons could have been waited out, starved out or even bombed or shelled out quite easily. But when their commanding officer, Colonel Oates, attempted to bypass the deadly area and do as earlier units had done, march into Dublin around Beggars Bush Barracks, Lowe personally forbade the diversion. He wanted a full frontal assault; the rebels could and should be cleared out. When the brigade officer, Colonel Maconchy, contacted Lowe on the telephone and warned him that it would cost reinforcements and heavy casualties, Lowe still insisted that the position must be taken at all costs.

Taken it finally was. Malone and his Peter the Painter revolver eventually succumbed to vastly superior numbers. By then the engagement certainly deserved to be regarded as a Thermopylae. Malone died at his post, but Grace managed to escape in the darkness. He hid in a woodshed for three days before being captured. The Parochial Hall Garrison was also caught trying to escape as fire intensified on the Hall. Then the British managed to bring a machine gun to bear on Clanwilliam House from the belfry of a church in Haddington Road. The combined effect of its fire, hand grenades and superiority in manpower of in excess of a hundred to one eventually told. By eight in the evening, after a day without food or water, almost continuously firing and under fire, the little garrison was decimated. One of them, Patrick Doyle, called out: 'Boys, isn't this a great day for Ireland? Did I ever think I'd live to see a day like this. Shouldn't we be all grateful to the good God that He's allowed us to take part in a fight like this?' He was shot dead as he finished speaking.

The defenders tried to make up for his loss by dressing a dressmaker's dummy with his hat and jacket and placing it near a window. One by one, the garrison was being killed off. But when someone outside called out 'surrender', Reynolds replied with a fusillade and told the survivors not to worry: 'We'll have more men and plenty of ammunition soon...' He was killed shortly afterwards. The survivors made their way out of the back of the now-blazing house, leaving dead men still apparently guarding the windows. Some, however, must still have been alive to judge from Redmond-Howard's description of the final assault as the Tommies hurled hand grenades into the house:[54]

There was a 'Crash! Crash!' as the windows burst with the concussion, and within a few seconds the sky was lit up with the flames of the burning houses and the air rent with the screams of the Sinn Feiners as they faced cold steel. It was a ghastly scene. The smell of roasting flesh was still around the blazing building at ten o'Clock.

Three of the survivors, William Ronan and the Walshe brothers climbed over garden walls until they eventually found an empty basement flat where they put on clothes of all sorts including women's, and thus disguised, got away. The temper of the Dublin public was still that which had offered food and drink to the Tommies eight hours earlier. One of the Clanwilliam men, the wounded James Doyle, was set upon by a crowd as he literally staggered along. He was lucky enough to get away and to collapse near a friendly house into which he was carried and treated for his wounds. Meanwhile, in Mount Street Colonel Maconchy, having carried out General Lowe's orders, sat atop his horse riding through lines of British soldiers with fixed bayonets, while behind the bayonets massed crowds cheered and hailed the conquering hero.

Between them, Malone's men had accounted for four British officers killed, fourteen wounded and 215 other ranks killed and wounded. De Valera, of course, had taken no direct part in this action. His stronghold had been bypassed as that of Mount Street should have been. Nevertheless, not so very long after Maconchy's triumphal progression, the Dublin crowds would be cheering de Valera, the commander of the Mount Street men. Seeing the flames and hearing the bomb explosions and fierce fighting, neither de Valera nor his men realised that they had been bypassed and waited for an attack that never came. The strain told on de Valera.

He refused to sleep and rushed around giving orders which he frequently then countermanded. He ordered a retreat from his bakery headquarters to the railway, which had a higher elevation. However, this also afforded a frightening better view of the fires now consuming Dublin and had a demoralising effect on his men. He changed his mind and ordered his men to quit the railway and reoccupy the bakery, which of course could easily have been taken by the British in the meantime had they known about his evacuation. He did make one decision during the week which probably saved the lives of several of his men. He caused a green flag to be erected on a high unoccupied building so that when the British commenced shelling that position, they imagined this to be his command post and concentrated their fire on the empty building.

But his appearance tended to have an unsettling effect on his men. As he moved about giving contradictory orders, a tall, green, uniformed figure set off by long red socks, the Volunteers feared that they might lose their sanity. One Volunteer did so, shot a comrade and had to be clubbed unconscious himself. Once de Valera did yield to pressure and lay down to sleep after refusing to do so for days, saying: 'I can't trust the men – they leave their posts or fall asleep if I don't watch them'. This was a somewhat startling judgement on the fortitude of the men under his command. Malone and his men, after all, had no contact with him and received no reinforcements from him during the week.

However, he tossed and turned in obvious agitation and sat bolt upright, eyes staring, crying out: 'Set fire to the railway, set fire to the railway!' He then ordered that an attempt be made to set fire to Westland Row Station and to some rolling stock with the aid of newspapers dipped in whiskey.

This order was ultimately countermanded and the fire put out. But the memory of the railway obviously abided with him, because many years later when he had become President of Ireland, he confided a revealing anecdote to a friend of mine, the late Sean J. White. The scholarly White, in addition to being the head of Public Relations for the State Transport Company, *Coras Iompair Eireann*, was a fluent Irish speaker and was thus always chosen to accompany de Valera on his official journeys. Speaking in Irish, de Valera told White of an occasion during the occupation of the railway when he was overcome by tiredness and lay down in an empty carriage and went asleep. When he awoke, he thought he had died and gone to heaven. All he could see above him were angels and cherubs. After a while, he realised there was a very good reason for this. He was looking at angels and cherubs. He had unknowingly gone to sleep in the Royal Coach – a coach which he later used himself on his Presidential journeys.

In the conditions of Easter Week it did not seem possible that de Valera or any of his colleagues would ever survive to make train journeys anywhere. Michael Collins later wrote this assessment of the fighting and of his leaders:[55]

Although I was never actually scared in the GPO I was – and others also – witless enough to do the most stupid things. As the flames and heat increased so apparently did the shelling. Machine-gun fire made escape more or less impossible. Not that we wished to escape. No man wished to budge. In that building, the defiance of our men, and the gallantry, reached unimaginable proportions.

It is so easy to fault the actions of others when their particular actions have resulted in defeat. I want to be quite fair about this – the Easter Rising – and say how much I admired the men in the ranks and the womenfolk thus engaged. But at the same time – as it must appear to others also – the actions of the leaders should not pass without comment. They have died nobly at the hands of the firing squads. So much I grant. But I do not think the Rising week was an appropriate time for the issue of memoranda couched in poetic phrases, nor of actions worked out in a similar fashion. Looking at it from the inside (I was in the GPO), it had the air of a Greek tragedy about it, the illusion being more or less completed with the issue of the before-mentioned memoranda. Of Pearse and Connolly I admire the latter the most. Connolly was a realist. Pearse the direct opposite. There was an air of earthy directness about Connolly. It impressed me. I would have followed him through hell had such action been necessary. But I honestly doubt very much if I would have followed Pearse – not without some thought anyway.

I think chiefly of Tom Clarke and MacDiarmada. Both built on the best foundations. Ireland will not see another Sean MacDiarmada.

These are sharp reflections. On the whole I think the Rising was bungled terribly, costing many a good life. It seemed at first to be well-organised, but afterwards became subjected to panic decisions and a great lack of very essential organisation and co-operation.

The first sample (I am assuming that Collins exempted the Declaration of the Republic from his strictures) of the spate of memoranda 'couched in poetic phrases' to which Collins referred emanated from Pearse the day after the Rising began. It said:

The Provisional Government to the Citizens of Dublin:

The Provisional Government of the Irish Republic salutes the Citizens of Dublin on the momentous occasion of the proclamation of a SOVEREIGN INDEPENDENT IRISH STATE now in the course of being established by Irishmen in arms.

The Republican forces hold the lines taken up at Twelve noon on Easter Monday, and nowhere, despite fierce and almost continuous attacks of the British troops have the lines been broken through. The country is rising in answer to Dublin's call, and the final achievement of Ireland's freedom is now, with God's help, only a matter of days. The valour, self-sacrifice and discipline of Irish men and women are about to win for our country a glorious place among the nations.

Ireland's honour has already been redeemed; it remains to vindicate her wisdom and her self-control.

All citizens of Dublin who believe in the right of their Country to be free will give their allegiance and their loyal help to the Irish Republic. There is work for everyone; for the men in the fighting line, and for the women in the provision of food and first aid. Every Irishman and Irish woman worthy of the name will come forward to help their common country in this her supreme hour.

Able-bodied citizens can help by building barricades in the streets to oppose the advance of the British troops. The British troops have been firing on our women and on our Red Cross. On the other hand, Irish regiments in the British Army have refused to act against their fellow countrymen.

The Provisional Government hopes that its supporters – which means the vast bulk of the people of Dublin – will preserve order and self-restraint. Such looting as has already occurred has been done by the hangers-on of the British Army. Ireland must keep her new honour unsmirched.

We have lived to see an Irish Republic proclaimed. May we live to establish it firmly, and may our children and our children's children enjoy the happiness and prosperity which freedom will bring.

Signed on behalf of the Provisional Government.
P. H. Pearse
Commanding in Chief of the Forces of the Irish
Republic and President of the Provisional Government

Of course the country did not rise and there was no mutiny in the British Army. In fact, as indicated, the Dublin Fusiliers was one of the units which took an active part in crushing the rebellion, as did individual ex-Volunteers who had joined the British Army in answer to Redmond's call, in some cases having assisted in the Howth gun running.

The noose tightened on the city and heavy artillery shells began to rain down accompanied by machine gun and rifle fire. One of the methods used by the British to get close to rebel positions was in anticipation of tank warfare. A

Colonel Portal is credited with being the brains behind a scheme which procured two large iron boilers from the Guinness Brewery, cut holes in them with dummy holes painted alongside, and then mounted them on motor lorries, so that eighteen soldiers at a time could be transported in noisy, uncomfortable safety through slum streets made deadly by sniper fire. Safety, that is, until the rebels cottoned on to the idea of firing not at the boilers but the drivers of the trucks. Inside the GPO the situation became increasingly desperate. The centre of Dublin became an inferno. All around the GPO as well as on the opposite side of Sackville Street, business premises were on fire. At night people standing on vantage points like Killiney Hill and Howth Head could clearly see Nelson standing atop his pillar, nine or ten miles away.

With a view not to depriving sightseers of a landmark, but to removing a symbol of British imperialism, the rebels made several efforts to blow up Nelson's Pillar, but it survived these virtually unscathed. (Ironically enough, fifty years later when the country was at peace, the IRA decided to commemorate the Rising by making a successful onslaught on the Pillar.) The incessant bombardment made communication between the rebel strongpoints almost impossible.

As the week wore on, buildings facing the GPO were mistakenly evacuated when an order from Connolly to cease fire was mistranslated. However, when he called for Volunteers to reoccupy them, a party of thirteen Volunteers braved the flames and the bullets to retake some of the evacuated positions so that resistance could be put up should the British mount a charge across O'Connell Street.

Only eight men managed to survive the crossing. Connolly did not expect his men to take risks which he would not take himself. Apart from directing the fire from inside the GPO, he constantly went outside the building, checking barricades or directing men into sniper positions.

Eventually, however, he paid the price for his courage. A ricocheting bullet caught him in the ankle as he stepped from his sheltered position in Middle Abbey Street to urge on a party of Volunteers. He had crawled over 100 yards in agony before he was spotted from the GPO and carried to relative safety. Here, his worst danger came from a medical student who had failed to qualify as a doctor after ten years of study. He made up a solution of chloroform which was so weak that the doctor who eventually did tend to him, Captain Mahony, a British officer whom the rebels had captured, later judged that it would have taken a lake of that solution to render Connolly unconscious. When Connolly came to, he told Mahony that he was the best thing the Volunteers had captured all week.[56] But both Connolly and the Rising were now in a desperate state. His bodyguard, Harry Walpole, recorded that during the night he heard Connolly cry out: 'Oh God, did ever a man suffer more for his country?'

He passed a wretched sleepless night in great pain from his injury, as did Plunkett, who nevertheless roused himself from his mattress to help direct the fighting while Connolly was recovering from the effects of shock and chloroform. On the morning of 28 April, Connolly insisted that despite his suffering, he must 'give confidence to the Garrison'. He was placed on an iron bed and manhandled into the front hall where despite his obvious wounds, his appearance was a major morale booster. Hearing that he had reappeared, Harry Walpole made his way to his bedside and lit a cigarette for him. Connolly put down his detective story, took a deep drag and commented: 'A book like this, plenty of rest and an insurrection – all at the same time. This certainly is Revolution de luxe.'

Sackville Street became an inferno. Landmark Dublin businesses collapsed on to the roadway in an avalanche of flames and smoking debris. Included in the debris were the molten remnants of the huge quantities of gold and silver ornaments, once kept safely in the jewellers Hopkins & Hopkins. Hoytes Oilworks just opposite the GPO shook the walls with a terrifying explosion as thousands of oil drums exploded simultaneously over Sackville Street. The heat inside the GPO became so intense that when hoses were turned on the window barricades to prevent them igniting, the water immediately turned into steam. As Plunkett looked out on the flames he commented: 'It's the first time it's happened since Moscow – the first time a Capital has been burnt since then.'

Desmond Ryan, Pearse's literary executor, who has left behind some of the best writings on Easter Week, described how Pearse reacted to the destruction. He praised The O'Rahilly for his gallantry in electing to share this Gethsemane with them, even though he had been against the Rising. He said:

Well, when we're all wiped out, people will blame us for everything, I suppose, and condemn us. Yet if it hadn't been for this protest, the war would have ended and nothing would have been done. After a few years people will see the meaning of all we tried to do... You know, Emmet's insurrection is as nothing to this. They will talk of Dublin in the future as one of the splendid cities – as they speak today of Paris. Dublin's name will be glorious for ever!

As he spoke, two major Dublin premises, Clery's Department Store and the Imperial Hotel, collapsed with a horrendous crashing sound, sending great gouts of fire hundreds of feet into the sky. Pearse fell silent, but Ryan noted how all around them the rebels drowned out the roar of the flames and of the guns with the song that became the Irish national anthem, *The Soldiers Song*:

> *Soldiers are we,*
> *Whose lives are pledged to*
> *Ireland. ....!*

The pledges were about to be called in. But first Pearse and Connolly issued more proclamations, which given the circumstances, might at first sight be taken as merely vying with each other in grandiloquence and unreality. However, apart from any morale-boosting effect they may have had on their soldiers at the time, they were to form a powerful part of the armoury of 1916 publications with which Sinn Fein protagonists were to advance on their opponents in the wake of the Rising. Connolly then dictated the following which reached Pearsian heights in its disregard for the reality of the rebels' situation:

Army of the Irish Republic (Dublin Command)
Headquarters, April 28th, 1916

To Soldiers,

This is the fifth day of the establishment of the Irish Republic, and the flag of our country still floats from the most important buildings in Dublin, and is gallantly protected by the officers and Irish soldiers in arms throughout the country. Not a day passes without seeing fresh postings of Irish soldiers eager to do battle for the old cause. Despite the utmost vigilance of the enemy we have been able to get information telling us how the manhood of Ireland, inspired by our splendid action, are gathering to offer up their lives, if necessary, in this same holy cause. We are here hemmed in because the enemy feels in this building is to be found the heart and inspiration of our great movement.

Let us remind you of what you have done. For the first time in 700 years the flag of free Ireland floats triumphantly in Dublin City.

The British Army, whose exploits we are forever having dinned into our ears, which boasts of having stormed the Dardanelles and the German lines on the Marne, behind their artillery and machine-guns are afraid to advance to the attack or storm any positions held by our forces. The slaughter they have suffered in the last few days has totally unnerved them, and they dare not attempt again an infantry attack on our positions. Our Commandants around us are holding their own.

Commandant Daly's splendid exploit in capturing Linenhall Barracks we all know. You must know also that the whole population, both clergy and laity, of this district are united in his praises. Commandant MacDonagh is established in an impregnable position reaching from the walls of

Dublin Castle to Redmond's Hill and from Bishop Street to
Stephen's Green.

(In Stephen's Green, Commandant Mallin holds the
College of Surgeons, one side of the square, a portion of the
other side and dominates the whole Green and all its
entrances and exits.) Commandant de Valera stretches in a
position from the Gas works to Westland Row, holding
Boland's Bakery, Boland's Mills, Dublin South-Eastern
Railway Works and dominating Merrion Square.

Commandant Kent holds the South Dublin Union and
Guinness's Buildings in Marrowbone Lane and controls
James Street and district.

On two occasions the enemy effected a lodgement and
were driven out with great loss.

The men of North County Dublin are in the field, have
occupied all the Police barracks in the district, destroyed all
the telegram system on the Great Northern Railway up to
Dundalk, and are operating against the trains of the Midland
and Great Western.

Dundalk has sent 200 men to march upon Dublin, and in
the other parts of the North our forces are active and growing.

In Galway Captain Mellowes, fresh after his escape from
an English prison, is in the field with his men. Wexford and
Wicklow are strong and Cork and Kerry are equally acquitting themselves creditably. (We have every confidence that
our Allies in Germany and kinsmen in America are straining
every nerve to hasten matters on our behalf.)

As you know, I was wounded twice yesterday, and am
unable to move about, but have got my bed moved into the
firing line, and with the assistance of your officers, will be
just as useful to you as ever.

Courage, boys, we are winning, and in the hour of our victory, let us not forget the splendid women who have everywhere stood by us and cheered us on. Never had man or woman a grander cause, never was a cause more grandly served.

(Signed)

James Connolly
Commandant-General
Dublin Division.

One of the few factual statements in that message was that concerning Commandant Edward Daly who was in charge of the Four Courts, Church Street, North King Street area which saw some of the bitterest fighting and, as we shall see, worst incidents of the Rising. Daly's men did capture the Linenhall Barracks in a daring operation. Daly subsequently had it set alight, but then fearing that the flames would spread because the fire brigade was refusing to turn out, ordered his men to fight the blaze. This they did, under sustained fire from the military. Daly also saw to it that people in his area were fed by overseeing the distribution of bread, the traditional staple diet of the poor, from Monk's Bakery which he had taken over. On the day that Connolly issued his statement a man arrived in Dublin whose orders would ensure that the fighting in Daly's Command area would have consequences which would live in Irish memories long after the Rising ended. Those orders would also directly ensure that Daly and a number of others would not live long after the Rising ended.

The man was General Sir John Grenfell Maxwell, KCB, KCMG, whose career had been blighted because he was apportioned some of the blame for the slaughter of allied troops, including many Irish soldiers, by the Turks at Gallipoli. Maxwell had now been offered the opportunity of resuscitating his career by accepting the post of General Officer commanding all forces in Ireland, with authority to take any steps he deemed necessary to suppress the rebellion. This in effect placed Ireland under his control and rendered Birrell and Wimborne subject to his orders. When he arrived in Dublin in the small hours of that Friday morning, the place looked like an *après*-bombardment European city. Wrecked buildings and fires abounded as did artillery and rifle fire. Prompt action was called for. He issued a Proclamation:

> The most vigorous measures will be taken by me to stop the loss of life and damage to property which certain misguided persons are causing in their armed resistance to the law. If necessary I shall not hesitate to destroy any buildings within any area occupied by the rebels and I warn all persons within the area specified below, and now surrounded by HM troops, forthwith to leave such area.

The warren of little streets behind the Four Courts, the North King Street area, was 'surrounded by HM troops'. But even if the inhabitants had chosen to leave their tenement homes, which they had refused to do all week, and assuming that any of them ever heard of Maxwell's Proclamation, the steadily increasing fighting would have ruled out any such attempt now. Their homes appeared to be the only safe haven in a world turned nightmarish. This would prove to be a mistaken belief, ironically, chiefly after the fighting ended.

Artillery shells had wreaked such havoc that the rebels could no longer control the fire in the GPO. Connolly was reduced to appointing a fifteen-year-old boy, Sean MacLoughlin, as a Commandant, an unusually brave and resourceful boy, but a fifteen-year-old nonetheless. In the evening it was decided to evacuate. The O'Rahilly led thirty men in a charge down Moore Street, twenty-one of whom became casualties, including O'Rahilly himself. Though mortally wounded, he managed to survive long enough to write a farewell letter to his wife, explaining why he had joined the Rising. The other leaders, Pearse, Connolly, Plunkett, Clarke and MacDermott managed to get to a fish shop, O'Hanlon's, at No. 16, Moore Street.

Here a plan was agreed which would have entailed burrowing through a maze of streets in the area until they reached the Four Courts to link up with the garrison there for a final stand. It was daring and would certainly have entailed the loss of both Volunteer and civilian life, but it would have prolonged the Revolution. To the Provisional Government every hour gained, every shell fired, every building destroyed, indicated that the protest in arms was serious, that Ireland had a case, and that it should be heard at the Peace Conference. It has been suggested that Pearse decided to surrender, however, because he witnessed an incident which decided him against further fighting at the cost of civilian lives. A Moore Street publican carrying a white flag along with his wife and daughter, were cut down by the military as they fled the burning public house.

In a letter to his mother two days before he was shot Pearse wrote:[57] 'My own opinion was in favour of one more desperate sally before opening negotiations, but I yielded to

the majority, and I think now the majority were right'.
He ordered a ceasefire. Elizabeth O'Farrell, who had acted
as a nurse all through the GPO fighting, was provided
with a makeshift Red Cross insignia and a white flag,
and instructed to inform the British that Pearse wanted
to talk terms. The first waving of the flag provoked rifle
fire from the British but the courageous young woman
persisted and at 12.45 p.m. on Saturday, 29 April, 1916 she
stepped out into the open street and walked towards the
soldiers.

The initial British response was not very reassuring. The
first British officer she spoke to, a Colonel Hodgkin, began by
telling her merely to go back and bring the other two women
with the Volunteer party to safety with her. Then he remarked:
'I suppose this will have to be reported', a not unreasonable
supposition in the circumstances. The Commanding Officer,
Colonel Portal, the armoured car inventor, and Ms O'Farrell,
then conducted the following dialogue.

O'FARRELL: The Commandant of the Irish Republican
   Army wishes to treat with the Commandant of the British
   forces in Ireland.
PORTAL: The Irish Republican Army? – the Sinn Feiners,
   you mean.
O'FARRELL: No, the Irish Republican Army they call them-
   selves and I think that is a very good name, too.
PORTAL: Will Pearse be able to be moved on a stretcher?
O'FARRELL: Commandant Pearse doesn't need a stretcher.
PORTAL (turning to another officer): Take that Red Cross off
   her and bring her over there and search her – she's a spy.

However, General Lowe, who combined the sending of men to the slaughter with an old-world courtesy, behaved in a more gentlemanly fashion. He sent her back to Pearse in a motor car to Moore Street with a note and a verbal message to the effect that there would be no negotiation, only an unconditional surrender. Lowe's only concession was that he would accept the surrender of the other commandants. After surrendering to Lowe, who was accompanied by his son John, Pearse was taken before General Maxwell at the headquarters of the Irish Command at Parkgate Street. Here he had what Maxwell's biographer has described as a 'short and stern' interview with the General, who demanded and got the instrument of surrender (see picture section).

After signing the order, Pearse was locked in a sitting room (which later became the office of the Irish Minister for Defence) with Lowe's aide, Major de Courcy Wheeler, who was ordered to shoot him if he tried to escape. However, de Courcy Wheeler wrote later, Pearse merely 'smiled at me across the table and did not seem in the least perturbed'. De Courcy Wheeler also took part in the last act of Edward Daly's surrender. The British were impressed with Daly's bearing and allowed him to march from the Four Courts at the head of his men, carrying their rifles to the surrender point, the Gresham Hotel in Sackville Street. When Lowe saw the weapons he told de Courcy Wheeler to order the men to lay down the guns. Daly, however, intercepted the command, stepping forward as if he were on parade and issuing normal drill instructions. The men obeyed him smartly and de Courcy Wheeler was so impressed that involuntarily he exchanged salutes with Daly. Watching his aide salute, Lowe was heard to exclaim:[58] 'God! Saluting a rebel!'

It took some time for the surrender order to be accepted. Connolly countersigned Pearse's order when it was brought to him in the Red Cross Hospital in Dublin Castle, but wrote on it: 'I agree to these conditions for the men only under my command in the Moore Street District and for the men in the St Stephen's Green Command'. Two priests had to visit Pearse in his cell in Arbour Hill Detention barracks on Sunday to get a copy, dated 30 April, for the men in the Church Street area. Ashe sent Richard Mulcahy under safe conduct to the cell also the same day and only surrendered when Mulcahy returned to tell him that Pearse had said it was no use holding out. When two Wexford Volunteers, Sean Etchingham and Seamus Doyle were brought to him later he gave them another copy of the surrender order whispering to them to hide their arms in safe places. 'They will be needed later', he said. When Elizabeth O'Farrell presented de Valera with the order he at first refused to accept it, fearing that it was a trap. Some of his hesitancy was due to the fact that rumours of captured soldiers being shot out of hand on the Western Front were common in Dublin. In his case, the sort of slaughter which precipitated such action had occurred, not on the far away battlefield, but a few hundred yards away under his command. Moreover, his men had not been in action and wanted to fight on, but they were persuaded that surrender was the only way to spare de Valera's life. He was not fully convinced that it would be spared, and took along a captured cadet, G. F. Mackay, to witness his surrender, so that at least he would not be shot out of hand. He told his captors:[59] 'Do what you like with me, but I demand proper treatment for my men'.

When the men realised that de Valera had surrendered,

they took some convincing before they themselves gave up, emerging from the bakery still carrying their rifles and refusing to carry a white flag which had to be borne by a Red Cross worker. Nevertheless, despite these ambiguities, de Valera would be remembered as the only Commandant of 1916 to survive the firing squads. Dubliners would remember the flag on the tower incident and a remark he made as he was marched to a holding centre at the Ballsbridge Showground (the Spring Show had at last come to an end). Passing No. 25 Northumberland Road where the gallant Malone had died, he looked at the people coming out of their homes to bring tea to the soldiers guarding him and his men and said bitterly: 'If you had only come out with hayforks.'

Where the GPO garrison were concerned Murphy's law continued to operate. The fine weather with which the Rising opened turned to drizzle at its close as the prisoners were corralled on the open ground behind the Rotunda where the Volunteers had been founded. Another ironic choice of location by the British was the taking over of Tom Clarke's shop as a centre of operations. Initially, Michael Collins had derived some comfort from the fact that the tricolour somehow survived the holocaust and still flew over the GPO, but that piece of symbolism proved inedaquate to ward off the effects of the psychological let-down after the surrender. To this, the strain of the week, hunger and in particular, thirst, and the damp and depression of a sleepless night in the open were added to the humiliations imposed on the prisoners by the officer in charge, a Captain Lee-Wilson.

He had some of the prisoners stripped, among them Tom

Clarke, and paraded on the steps of the Rotunda for the benefit of the nurses looking out of the adjoining hospital windows. Clarke had sustained a bullet wound in the elbow during pistol practice and Captain Lee-Wilson ordered that the bandage be torn off, opening the wound. Michael Collins tried to comfort the older man, attempting to keep him warm during the night by wrapping his arms around him. When the prisoners were eventually ordered to march to a detention centre a couple of miles away Lee-Wilson ordered that Sean MacDermott's stick be taken from him. Polio had rendered MacDermott unable to walk without it and he had to be carried towards his fate by a comrade. One of Lee-Wilson's ukases was an order that the prisoners be forced to relieve themselves where they lay. Michael Collins survived to relieve himself for all this in another fashion some years later by having the same Lee-Wilson shot.

The Rising had killed and severely wounded some 1350 people. The centre of Dublin was gutted. Approximately 61,000 square yards of buildings were destroyed. Damage was estimated at some £2,500,000 Sterling in the values of the day. On top of this, approximately one-third of the city's population had to be given public relief. The interruption of food supplies meant that throughout the week the threat of starvation had hung over the city. The initial outrage that greeted all this was hardly surprising. Dubliners, some with husbands and relatives at the Front, had hooted and jeered at the prisoners as they were marched through the city they had shattered. Vegetables were thrown at them, even the contents of chamberpots, as they passed by, dirty, weary, hungry, yet still with sufficient defiance in their ranks for some to continue singing their 'scaffold songs'. The metamorphosis of this band of bungling idealists into a host of heroes is one of the most amazing transformations in Irish history.

General Maxwell played a pivotal role in the transformation. He later prepared a memo for Asquith explaining his actions:

> In view of the gravity of the Rebellion and its connection with German intrigue and propaganda and in view of the great loss of life and destruction of property resulting there-from, the General Officer Commanding in Chief Irish Command, has found it imperative to inflict the most severe sentences on the organisers of this detestable Rising and on the Commanders who took an actual part in the actual fighting which occurred. It is hoped that these examples will be sufficient to act as a deterrent to intriguers and to bring home to them that the murder of Her Majesty's subjects or other acts calculated to imperil the safety of the realm will not be tolerated.

This policy created a public relations disaster. The day after the surrender, prisoners were marched to Richmond Barracks where they were screened by the 'G Men' (the political wing of the police force), for court-martial and the death sentence. For reasons we shall shortly explore, the conduct of the actual court-martial itself also angered public opinion. As can be seen from the following list, those executed included not only the leaders of the Rising but some of those who had fought most bravely:

P. H. Pearse	shot in Dublin	May 3
Tom Clarke	shot in Dublin	May 3

Thomas MacDonagh	shot in Dublin	May 3
Joseph Plunkett	shot in Dublin	May 4
Edward Daly	shot in Dublin	May 4
William Pearse	shot in Dublin	May 4
Michael O'Hanrahan	shot in Dublin	May 4
John MacBride	shot in Dublin	May 5
Eamonn Kent	shot in Dublin	May 8
Michael Mallin	shot in Dublin	May 8
Con Colbert	shot in Dublin	May 8
Sean Heuston	shot in Dublin	May 8
Sean MacDermott	shot in Dublin	May 12
James Connolly	shot in Dublin	May 12
Thomas Kent	shot in Cork	May 9
Roger Casement	Hanged in Pentonville Prison (London)	August 3

In terms of the daily slaughter on the Western Front the totals were not high, but coming against the background of Conservative and Unionist opposition to Home Rule, those executions changed Irish history. The rebellion was not even over when the *Glasgow Observer* of 29 April, 1916, after making some ritual condemnations of the Rising, went on to say:

No Irish Nationalist should grovel to his British neighbour over what happened in Dublin on Monday. It was simply the consequences of what happened earlier at Larne when the associates and followers of Sir Edward Carson flouted and defied the law of the land, held up its legal guardians and engaged in military operations. ...Hand in glove with them in the lawlessness was Mr Bonar Law, now a Coalition Minister and Sir F. E. Smith, then Carson's 'galloper', now Attorney General for England. The Carsonite Rebellion, for that is what it was, was not merely tolerated and utilised by the whole Tory Party…Larne begat Dublin.

On 6 May, Maxwell had been summoned before the Cabinet and warned that no woman was to be executed (Asquith, it seems, had already vetoed Countess Markievicz's execution) and that only the ringleaders and proved murderers should be shot. But as the days passed, the executions continued, ordered in secret court martials, which gave the public no inkling of who had been sentenced or who was next, and spread out in a manner which readers may assess for themselves from the dates given above. With every firing squad volley, more and more people came to agree with the *Glasgow Observer*'s opinion: 'Larne begat Dublin'. The swing in public opinion saved de Valera's life. He had been due to be shot after Connolly, but was one of those whose sentence was commuted to life imprisonment. No one denied that the rebels had fought bravely and fairly. Asquith began to find himself under pressure from public opinion to halt the executions. Irish Americans were particularly denunciatory and England desperately needed American assistance in the war. Asquith himself displayed no anti-Irish feeling. In a remarkably fair-minded assessment for any Englishman in the circumstances, let alone a Prime Minister, he told the House of Commons:[60]

> So far as the great body of the insurgents is concerned I have no hesitation in saying in public that they conducted themselves with great humanity which contrasted very much to

their advantage with some of the so-called civilised enemies
with which we are fighting in Europe. That admission I
gladly make and the House will gladly hear it. They were
young men; often lads. They were misled, almost uncon-
sciously I believe, into this terrible business. They fought
very bravely and did not resort to outrage.

Well aware of what was happening to Irish public opinion, the
Irish Parliamentary Party appealed both publicly and
privately that the executions be stopped. In the House of
Commons John Dillon pointed out to the Prime Minister that
it was the first rebellion in Irish history in which the people
had aided the Government but that the Government response
had been martial law and executions: 'It is not murderers
who are being executed,' he said; 'it is insurgents who
fought a clean fight, a brave fight'. Privately John Redmond
warned Asquith that the executions were destroying what
was left of the credibility of his party. Even within his
own ranks the cracks were showing. Dillon, for example,
visited the prisoners after they were transferred to jails in
England and congratulated them on the fight they had
put up. In a notably prophetic and courageous protest, given
that he was living in wartime England, dependent on the
British public for his livelihood, George Bernard Shaw
wrote:[61]

My own view is that the men who were shot in cold blood,
after their capture or surrender, were prisoners of war, and
that it was therefore, entirely incorrect to slaughter them.
The relation of Ireland to Dublin Castle is, in this respect,
precisely that of the Balkan States to Turkey, to Belgium or

the City of Lille to the Kaiser, and of the United States to Great Britain.

Until Dublin Castle is superseded by a National Parliament and Ireland voluntarily incorporated with the British Empire, as Canada, Australasia, and South Africa have been incorporated, an Irishman resorting to arms to achieve the independence of his country is doing only what Englishmen will do, if it be their misfortune to be invaded and conquered by the Germans in the course of the present war. Further, such an Irishman is as much in order morally in accepting assistance from the Germans, in his struggle with England, as England is in accepting the assistance of Russia in her struggle with Germany. The fact that he knows that his enemies will not respect his rights if they catch him, and that he must, therefore, fight with a rope round his neck, increases his risk, but adds in the same measure to his glory in the eyes of his compatriots and of the disinterested admirers of patriotism throughout the world. It is absolutely impossible to slaughter a man in this position without making him a martyr and a hero, even though the day before the rising he may have been only a minor poet. The shot Irishmen will now take their places beside Emmet and the Manchester Martyrs in Ireland, and beside the heroes of Poland and Serbia and Belgium in Europe; and nothing in Heaven or earth can prevent it…

The Military authorities and the English Government must have known that they were canonising their prisoners…

I remain an Irishman, and am bound to contradict any implication that I can regard as a traitor any Irishman taken in a fight for Irish Independence against the British Government, which was a fair fight in everything except the enormous odds my countrymen had to face.

There were, of course, other Irishmen who did not share Shaw's view. On the day that Kent and Mallin were shot James Craig rose in the House to ask Asquith: 'What steps had been taken to clear out members of the Sinn Fein Society from the Postal Service, Land Commission and other Government Departments?' A memorial was signed by 763 of Dublin's leading citizens, all of them Unionists, protesting against any interference with the discretion of the Commanders in Chief of the forces in Ireland and the operation of martial law. The *Irish Independent* and the *Irish Times* were both virulently hostile to the rebels, as was the *Irish Catholic*, which termed the Rising 'as criminal as it was insane... traiterous and treacherous'. Both the *Independent* and the *Irish Catholic* were owned by William Martin Murphy who had been Larkin and Connolly's principal opponent during the great lockout of 1913. On 10 May, after noting that some leaders were still awaiting sentence (including Connolly), the *Independent*'s leading article continued:

> When, however we come to some of the ringleader, instigators and fomentors not yet dealt with, we must make an exception. If these men are treated with too great leniency, they will take it as an indication of weakness on the part of the Government...let the worst of the rebels be singled out and dealt with as they deserve.

The *Irish Times* also wanted blood, thundering that the 'rapine and bloodshed of the past week must be punished with a severity which will make any repetition of them impossible for many years to come'.

In a classic display of loyalty not to the Crown, but the half-crown, on the day that MacBride was shot the Dublin Chamber of Commerce wrote to Buckingham Palace protesting the loyalty of the Chamber to the Crown and its abhorrence of the action of 'a section of the community'. However, the Chamber averred that the acts of murder and carnage would not have occurred were it not for the 'gross and imponderable laxity, long continued' of the Irish Government. As a result, the Chamber had decided that 'rebuilding costs etc should be provided by the Imperial Treasury without delay...'

Later, on the Nationalist side, in his poem *Easter 1916*, Yeats summed up the feelings of the thoughtful, torn between a feeling that on the one hand had the Rising not occurred, the British might yet have played fair over Home Rule, and on the other a troubling recognition that now that it had occurred a whole new situation had been created:[62]

> *Was it needless death after all?*
> *For England may keep faith*
> *...MacDonagh and MacBride*
> *And Connolly and Pearse*
> *Now and in time to be,*
> *Wherever green is worn,*
> *Are changed, changed utterly:*
> *A terrible beauty is born.*

In an effort to see for himself what was happening Asquith visited Dublin and saw the prisoners in Richmond Barracks (now Griffith Barracks). He pronounced them 'very good-looking fellows with such lovely eyes' and ordered that they should be thoroughly screened to ensure that they really were involved in the Rising. By then it had become obvious that in the post-Rising round-up, the British had swooped on people who were not even Gaelic Leaguers never mind physical force men. Apart from the captured insurgents themselves more than double the number who had actually taken part in the Rising were rounded up. Asquith did attempt to introduce Home Rule, but his proposal that the Act should go into operation as the war raged nearly broke up the strongly Unionist coalition. One member, Lord Selborne, actually resigned and the form of Government which contributed so much to the outbreak of the Rising was reinstituted in August 1916 with Wimborne becoming Lord Lieutenant once more and H. E. Duke becoming Chief Secretary. The appointments further underlined the increasing irrelevance of Redmond's party, and for Nationalists at least, furnished an answer to Yeats's suggestion that England might 'keep faith'.

Birrell resigned as First Secretary after the Rising. Asquith received his resignation with tears in his eyes when Birrell came to him to say goodbye to office and his career in public life. A Royal Commission of Inquiry set up in London on 18 May under the chairmanship of Lord Hardinge of Penshurst, made a scapegoat of Birrell, stating that he was primarily responsible for the situation that was allowed to arise and for the outbreak which occurred. Nathan was blamed for not having sufficiently impressed upon the Chief Secretary during Birrell's prolonged absences in London, the necessity for a more active policy. Although he was removed from his post in Dublin, he went on to have a distinguished career in the public service.

A number of very different factors combined with the executions to complete the swing of post-Rising sentiment from the government to the insurgents. These were the effects of the Bowen-Colthurst murders, the North King Street atrocities and the refusal by the authorities to reveal the details of the in-camera court martials. Lurid accounts of these interacted with reports from the condemned prisoners, and their families' accounts of their last moments. Captain Bowen-Colthurst, a member of a prominent Anglo-Irish family and a former ADC to the previous Viceroy, Lord Aberdeen, ordered his men to shoot six innocent civilians, including the pacifist Francis Sheehy Skeffington, in and around Portobello Barracks, during the Rising.

The Army had been made aware of his conduct during the fighting but took no action to stop the Bowen-Colthurst murders, and then tried to cover up his actions. Major Sir Francis Vane, who raised the matter, lost his rank and was dismissed from the service. Sheehy Skeffington's widow complained to Asquith, who at first did not believe her, but after inspecting the Army's handiwork for himself in Dublin, apparently changed his mind. Bowen-Colthurst was court-martialled on 6 June, 1916, found guilty but insane and was sent to Broadmoor Criminal Asylum.

Bowen-Colthurst's court martial meant that the details of his atrocities entered the public domain. But it was not until the year 2001, as a result of New Labour's policy of openness and improved Anglo-Irish relations brought on by the Good Friday Agreement, that official papers[63] were released by the British Government confirming what had really happened in the Church Street–North King Street area. It had been generally suspected that fifteen civilians who lost their lives, allegedly during the fighting, were in fact, either shot or bayoneted after the ceasefire by members of the South Staffordshire Battalion.

The officer in charge of the troops, Colonel Taylor, refused to turn up at the inquest on two of the victims, Patrick Bealen and James Healy, whom the Staffordshires had buried in a cellar. Instead he forwarded a statement giving the Army's version of events. He could find no military witness who could throw light on how the men came to be killed: '...no persons were attacked by the troops other than those who were assisting the rebels and found with arms in their possession'. After giving examples of the difficulties encountered by the troops in the King Street, Linenhall Street, Church Street area, the Colonel pointed out that it had taken the troops:

> ...From 10 am on the 28th of April until 2 pm on the 29th to force their way along King St. from Linenhall St, a distance of some 150 yards only; and that the casualties sustained by the regiment (the great majority of which occurred at this spot) included five officers (including two Captains) wounded, eleven NCOs and men killed and twenty eight wounded.

'I am satisfied', he said, 'that during these operations the troops under my command showed great moderation and restraint under exceptionally difficult and trying circumstances'. What the Colonel's statement did not contain was the fact that Maxwell had personally ordered a Mount Street Bridge-type assault on the North King Street area and the troops used, the South Staffordshires, had been used to relieve those who had survived the Mount Street Bridge slaughter. Tough hard men from a tough hard place, the industrialised 'Black Country' of Midlands England, they marched from the tales of horror around Mount Street to write fresh chapters in North King Street. The subsequent fighting was amongst the most intense, if not the most intense, of the week, although the death toll was nothing like that of Mount Street. Fighting in close, dark, dirty confines through most of Friday night and Saturday morning, the troops rarely saw their enemies, but they saw the wounds which the Howth rifles inflicted.

They were further maddened when from behind a tenaciously held barricade, Daly's men began an impromptu concert, singing every 'scaffold song' they could think of. The troops would grit their teeth while the singing continued and then pour a ferocious volley towards the barricade when it ended. When the songs finally died away and the barricades were captured, the events which led to the Coroner's Court being held began. The Court refused to accept Colonel Taylor's statement. It said that it was satisfied that Patrick Bealen had been shot by the troops while 'an unarmed and unoffensive prisoner', and that if the military authorities 'had any inclination' they could produce the officer responsible. The authorities had no such inclination. Instead, one of the 'inquiries' which have traditionally followed British military transgression in Ireland was held. In this case it involved a huge identification parade at Straffan Camp, in which the entire Staffordshire Battalion was paraded, ostensibly, to enable the mothers and wives of the dead to identify the killers. Not surprisingly, none was identified. For example, two soldiers, a Sergeant Flood and a Corporal Bullock, who shot Bealen and Healy, had been shipped back to England. But it was obvious that more than two lowly NCOs had been involved in the murders.

In North King Street as in the Mount Street area, the military mindset was again a causative factor in the deaths. Here again, apart from Maxwell's ordering men into rifle fire from determined, barricaded rebels, operating in a warren of slum streets, General Lowe's orders were involved. As part of the Inquiry into the King Street killings, a secret report was prepared headed: 'Reports of courts of inquiry into cases of alleged shootings by soldiers'. Significantly, this hand-written description was crossed out by the Army lawyer charged with giving an opinion on the Inquiry, and the words 'Civilian shootings' added. The Inquiry documents contained the following damning facts:

> It is to be noted that Colonel Taylor, commanding the troops at this point, stated in evidence that he had attended the meeting with Brigadier-General Lowe, commanding the operations, and that General Lowe instructed him and other officers 'to the effect that no hesitation was to be shown in dealing with these rebels; that by their action they had placed themselves outside the law, and that they were not to be made prisoners'.

Referring to one of the cases, that of James Moore, the Investigating Law Officer wrote: 'I have no doubt, however, that if the evidence were published, there would be a demand that he (Sergeant Flood) should be tried for murder.'

Such considerations meant that none of the Staffordshires was so tried, nor were the facts presented at inquiries revealed. It was made clear that acting on the instructions of officers, people captured after the fighting had ceased were taken into yards and shot, and sometimes not even taken outside. Some of the evidence considered, both made this plain and indicated that the Staffordshires' actions may have been directed by their officers. The Inquiry included the testimony of a woman with regard to the case of Paddy Bealen:

> They brought Paddy down to the cellar again, and when they brought him down to the cellar they were told to shoot him. The woman said she asked the soldier: 'Why couldn't you let him off?' and he said: 'No, because the officers had seen him'. The woman continued: 'The soldier said that the man said his prayers and though he was not of his creed, the soldier helped him with his prayers, because he pitied him, and then they said they could not shoot him fair-faced. They told him to go to the foot of the stairs, and then they let bang at him'.

General Maxwell's appended comment on the North King Street cases was that the deceased met their deaths: 'in North King Street during heavy fighting and the responsibilities for their deaths rests with those resisting His Majesty's troops in the execution of their duty'. The legal expert, however, while agreeing that the facts of the North King Street Inquiry should not be made public because of the risk of generating 'hostile propaganda', noted: 'If the case had occurred in England, the right course would be to refer the cases to the D of PP [Department of Public Prosecution].' He went on:

> The root of the mischief was the military order to take no prisoners. This in itself may have been justifiable – but it should have been made clear that it did not mean that an unarmed rebel might be shot after he had been taken prisoner. Still less could it mean that a person taken on mere suspicion could be shot without trial.

But the emotion which the stories circulating around the North King Street killings enflamed was as nothing compared to the effect on the public imagination of the in-camera court martials and executions of the leaders. A number of Irish MPs sought to have the court martials made public, but the Adjutant General's decision was that:

> I do not hesitate to say that in the event of further disturbances in Ireland the difficulties of a successful and hasty suppression of rebellion or disturbance would be greatly increased and the interests of justice would be defeated if it were realized that the evidence of witnesses given in camera would, in all probability, after the Rebellion or disturbance had ceased, be given publicity.

Significantly, the AG commented that he had spoken to Sir John Maxwell on the subject, and that he was:

> ...Very strongly of opinion that publication would be not only a grave indiscretion but also a distinct breach of faith with those who took the decision that the court-martials

were to be held in camera. As I have before observed publication is in my opinion a complete admission that there was no justification for trial in camera (which in itself is a grave reflection upon the discretion of Sir John Maxwell) and as I have reason to believe that in certain cases the evidence was not too strong the inevitable results of publication would be that a certain section of the Irish community will urge that the sole reason for trial in camera was that the authorities intended to execute certain of the Sinn Feiners whether there was evidence against them or not. This is an argument which in my humble judgement would be extremely difficult to meet successfully if, as I think, the evidence in some of the cases was far from conclusive.

One of the arguments cited against publication of court martial proceedings which might indeed have led 'the Irish community' to believe that the authorities had their minds made up to execute the Sinn Fein leaders 'whether there was evidence against them or not' was the case of Eamonn Kent. It was pointed out that he had summonsed as one of his witnesses, Thomas MacDonagh. The court martial had been told that: 'Thomas MacDonagh was not available as a witness as he was shot that morning'. Another fact which would no doubt influence public opinion had they been able to read it was the Adjutant General's minute that: 'There is no legal justification for a Court Martial to be held in-camera, either in the Army Act, or in any regulation under the Defence of the Realm Act'. Not surprisingly, therefore, although Asquith had promised that copies of the proceedings of the courts would be published (*Hansard*, 24 October, 1916), the military authorities objected and succeeded in stalling publication until Asquith's coalition was replaced by that of Lloyd George. The increased Unionist representation in the Cabinet supported the cover-up, so that the foregoing details did not see the light of day until the New Year 2001.

What were circulated, however, in the wake of the Rising, sometimes in print (often tellingly inscribed on black-bordered memorial cards) or by word of mouth, were the accounts of relatives' last words with their condemned loved ones, and in some cases the statements of the accused at their flawed court martials. Every paragraph, every poem, became another potent draught of emotion from the, by now, free-flowing fountain of Irish Nationalism. Readers may judge for themselves the effects of the following selection of such valedictions.[64]

Connolly's daughter, Nora, who with her sister Ina had taken a message from Pearse to the Volunteers in the north that the Rising was to take place after all and had subsequently had to walk all the way from Dundalk (almost sixty miles) to Dublin, described her father's last moments in Dublin Castle. He was propped up in bed with his leg in a cage. Nora told him that her brother Rory, who had served under his father in the GPO, had been in prison. Connolly replied: 'So Rory was in prison, how long?' 'Eight days,' Nora replied. Connolly commented: 'He fought for his country, and has been imprisoned for his country, and he is not sixteen. He has had a great start in life, hasn't he, Nora?'

Nora was disconsolate both at her father's circumstances, and the fact that her northern mission had been in vain. She told him that she felt that she and her sister had done nothing. But Connolly hugged her, saying 'I think my little

woman did as much as any of us'. But he warned his
daughters that the fact of his being wounded would make no
difference to his fate, saying 'I remember what happened to
Scheepers in South Africa. He was wounded and they
executed him. That will have no effect on what they decide
to do, and that's that.' However, he assured his distraught
wife Lily that he was in no pain from his wound. Nora and
she were back in Dublin Castle three days later in the early
hours of 12 May. Nora's statement said:

We were wakened up at about one o'clock in the morning.
There was an Army lorry at the door and a British Officer
told us that the prisoner James Connolly wished to see his
wife and eldest daughter. Mama had an idea that he wasn't
well, that he had taken a turn for the worse. But it jumped to
my mind immediately. All the signatories of the Proclamation had been shot except Papa and Sean MacDermott. I
immediately said to myself: Papa is going to be shot. Anyway
we got ready. We went down and were taken in the Army
lorry right through town. (We were staying in William
O'Brien's house). It was an awfully queer eerie trip. There
was still a horrible smell of burning in O'Connell Street.
There was curfew and not a soul to be seen, not even a
soldier, until we came to the bridge. There were a number of
them there. When we were shown in, Papa said: 'Well Lily, I
suppose you know what this means?'

She said: 'Oh no Jim. Oh no!' and he said: 'Yes, lovie', and
then Mama broke down, sobbing, with her head on the bed.
Papa said: 'I fell asleep for the first time tonight and they
wakened me up at eleven and told me I was to die at dawn.'

Mama said: 'Oh no!' again, and then crying bitterly, 'But

your beautiful life, Jim, your beautiful life!' and he said: 'Wasn't it a full life, Lily, and isn't this a good end?' And she still cried and he said: 'Look Lily, please don't cry. You will unman me.'

So she tried to control herself. I was trying to control myself too. Then Papa said to me: 'Put your hand down on the bed.' So I put it down on the bed and he said: 'That's a copy of my statement to the Court Martial. Try and get it out.' The piece of paper was folded up very tightly – very small. So I took it anyway.

And we stayed there talking of little things. He was trying to plan a life for us after he'd be gone.

One thing he said to Mama I remember: 'The Socialists will never understand why I am here. They will all forget I am an Irishman.'

And then they told us the time was up and that we'd have to go. (He was to be shot at dawn.)

So Mama – we couldn't get Mama away from the bed and the nurse had to come and help her away.

And I went to the door. And then I went back again to him. And that was the last I saw of him.

Fifty years after the Rising, Clarke's widow Kathleen, who had been arrested after the Rising ended, gave me this account of her last meeting with her husband:[65]

I thought that in the morning we were likely to be brought before the commanding officer, so I had taken off my blouse and skirt and hung them up so that I wouldn't look too bad. There were six of us and we had only one blanket over us. We had been very annoyed at some young British soldiers coming to flirt with us. It was outrageous. Then an officer came and said I had permission to see my husband. 'My God, Kathleen', said one of the girls, 'what does that mean?' 'It means death,' I said. 'Oh no,' said the girl; Marie Perolz was her name. 'Look', said I, 'do you think that if the British government were going to send my husband on a journey any shorter than to the next world that they'd get an officer and a car out at midnight to go for me?' 'You're a stone', said the girl. I was.

We were stopped several times. There were snipers on a lot of rooftops and I didn't think we'd be let go on. But the officer showed his pass and we got through. Kilmainham was terrible. The conditions! There was a monk downstairs. He told me that my husband had put him out of the cell. There was no light in it, only a candle that a soldier held. [Other relatives' accounts noted that the prisoners did not have candles in their cells either, author.] 'Why did you surrender?' I asked Tom. 'I thought you were going to hold out for six months.' 'I wanted to', he said, 'but the vote went against me.' We talked about the future the whole time. I never saw him so buoyed up. He said that the first blow had been struck and Ireland would get her freedom but that she'd have to go through hell first.

I didn't cry. He had to face the ordeal by himself in the morning. If I broke down, it might have broken him down. I said, 'What did you do to that priest down there?' 'That damn fellow came in here', he said, 'and told me he'd give me confession if I'd admit that I was wrong and that I was sorry. I'm not sorry. I told him that I gloried in what I'd done.' I was expecting a baby but didn't tell him that in case it might upset him.

I asked an officer to have his body sent to me. He

hemmed and hawed and said he'd had no instructions about it. In the end he promised to do something. But they wrote to me afterwards that I couldn't have the body for burial. I walked home by myself from the Castle to Fairview. There was a smell of burning in the air. I had to walk in the middle of the road because things were falling off the roofs. In O'Connell Street a big policeman stopped me. When I told him who I was and where I was going, he said, 'You'd better go down Fairview, ma'am. There's some soldiers up at Parnell's Monument and they're not very nice.' I had to climb over a big pile of rubble in North Earl Street. The bricks were still hot. I never met a sinner all the way home.

I had sent the children down to Limerick and there was no one in the house. I don't drink but I had whiskey and brandy in the house in case any wounded were brought in. Now, I thought, I'll have one twenty-fours hours of oblivion; and I took out a bottle of port and filled myself out a glass. I thought it would be strong. But I was awake again in an hour.

My sister came up from the country, and that night a lorry came and took us to Kilmainham to say goodbye to my brother [Ned Daly]. I heard it coming before any of them and I said, 'It's coming to take us to Ned. He's going to be shot.' They thought I was going off my head. But a few minutes later we all heard it. Then it stopped outside the house. My sister didn't want me to go but I insisted. My brother was in uniform. He looked about eighteen. There was a group of officers outside the cell. They seemed to have some spite against him. The soldier holding the candle had been in my husband's firing party. He said that my husband was the bravest man he'd seen. I lost the baby about a week later. I don't know if it was a boy or a girl. I worked at the prisoners' fund even when I was in bed. It saved me from going mad. God must have put the idea into my head.

Before the end Pearse wrote a number of poems and letters[66] to his mother and to his brother Willie. He had no idea that Willie was to be executed, as though he took part in the Rising, he had not taken part in its planning and held no position of authority.

To my mother

My gift to you has been a gift of sorrow,
My one return for your rich gifts to me...

I would have brought royal gifts, and I have brought you
Sorrow and tears; and yet, it may be
That I have brought you something else besides –
The memory of my deed and of my name
A splendid thing which shall not pass away.
When men speak of me, in praise or in dispraise,
You will not heed, but treasure your own memory
Of your first son.

A mother speaks

Dear Mary, that didst see thy first-born Son
Go forth to die amid the scorn of men
For whom He died,
Receive my first-born son into thy arms,
Who also hath gone out to die for men,
And keep him by thee till I come to him.
Dear Mary, I have shared thy sorrow,
And soon shall share thy joy.

Pearse told his court martial:

When I was a child of ten I went down on my bare knees by my bedside one night and promised God that I should devote my life to an effort to free my country. I have kept that promise. As a boy and as a man I have worked for Irish freedom, first among all earthly things. I have helped to organise, to arm, to train, and to discipline my fellow countrymen to the sole end that, when the time came, they might fight for Irish freedom. The time, as it seemed to me, did come, and we went into the fight. I am glad we did. We seem to have lost. We have not lost. To refuse to fight would have been to lose; to fight is to win. We have kept faith with the past, and handed on a tradition to the future.

...I assume that I am speaking to Englishmen, who value their freedom and who profess to be fighting for the freedom of Belgium and Serbia. Believe that we, too, love freedom and desire it. To us it is more desirable than anything in the world. If you strike us down now, we shall rise again and renew the fight. You cannot conquer Ireland. You cannot extinguish the Irish passion for freedom. If our deed has not been sufficient to win freedom, then our children will win it by a better deed.

I repudiate the assertion of the prosecutor that I sought to aid and abet England's enemy. Germany is no more to me than England is. I asked and accepted German aid in the shape of arms and an expeditionary force. We neither asked for nor accepted Germany (sic) gold, nor had any traffic with Germany but what I state. My aim was to win Irish freedom: we struck the first blow ourselves, but should have been glad of an ally's aid.

Kilmainham Prison
2 May, 1916.

He wrote again to his mother on 1 May, saying:

> Our hope and belief is that the Government will spare the lives of all our followers, but we do not expect that they will spare the lives of the leaders. We are ready to die and we shall die cheerfully and proudly. Personally I do not hope or even desire to live, but I do hope and desire and believe that the lives of all our followers will be saved including the lives dear to you and me (my own excepted) and this will be a great consolation to me when dying.

He repeated the sentiments of the poem *To My Mother*:

> You must not grieve for all this. We have preserved Ireland's honour and our own. Our deeds of last week are the most splendid in Ireland's history. People will say hard things of us now, but we shall be remembered by posterity and blessed by unborn generations. You too will be blessed because you were my mother.

He wrote to Willie, saying: 'Dear old Willie, Goodbye and God bless you for all your faithful work for me at St Enda's and elsewhere. No one can ever have had so true a brother as you.' In his final letter to his mother he also referred to Willie saying: 'I hope and believe that Willie and the St Enda's boys will be safe.' His hopes were only realised for the St Enda's boys.

One of the most poignant events of the period was the wedding of the dying Joseph Plunkett to Grace Gifford in his Kilmainham cell shortly before he was executed. The details of the wedding were told and retold throughout

Ireland and abroad. Plunkett had become engaged the previous December intending to be married on Easter Sunday. MacNeill's orders countermanded not only the Rising but also the wedding. Grace and he agreed that if he were arrested she would marry him in prison. Like Kathleen Clarke and Mrs Pearse, Grace had a doubly agonised period of waiting for news, in the misplaced hope that the leaders would be treated as prisoners of war, because two of her loved ones were also shot. At dawn on Wednesday, 3 May, 1916, Grace's brother-in-law, Thomas MacDonagh, was executed in Kilmainham.

In her biography[67] Marie O'Neill graphically described how Grace reacted when she realised that her fiancé was also to be shot; she went out and bought a wedding ring. O'Neill writes that the jeweller was about to close for the day when 'a young and attractive lady, evidently of good social position' entered the shop. As she asked to see some wedding rings 'she tried to stifle convulsive sobs'. The jeweller, a Mr Stoker, remarked: 'You should not cry when you are going to be married.' She told him that she was 'Mr Plunkett's fiancée' and that she was to marry him that night before his execution. He tried to comfort her. She thanked him 'very courteously', chose the most expensive ring and paid for it in notes.

O'Neill quotes Grace's own account of how she went through the wedding dressed in 'a light frock made of a check fabric with white collars and cuffs' and a light brimmed hat:

I entered Kilmainham Jail on Wednesday 3rd of May at 6 pm and I was detained there till about 11.30 pm when I saw him

(Joe) for the first time in the prison chapel where the marriage was gone through and no speeches allowed. He was taken back to his cell and I left the prison with Father Eugene MacCarthy of James's Street. We tried to get shelter for the night and I was finally lodged at the house of Mr. Byrne – bell-founder – in James's Street. I went to bed at 1.30 and was wakened at 2 o'Clock by a policeman with a letter from the prison commandant – Major Lennon asking me to visit Joseph Plunkett. I was brought there in a motor and saw my husband in his cell, the interview occupying 10 minutes. During the interview the cell was packed with officers, and a sergeant who kept a watch in his hand and closed the interview by saying 'Your time is now up'.

This rather denatured account omits details such as the fact that on her first visit to the prison she spent the hours alone walking up and down a prison yard, while Plunkett remained confined to his cell. Or that the wedding took place in darkness (the gas supply failed) apart from one candle held by a soldier. Two soldiers carrying rifles acted as witnesses. Plunkett, who had been detained in the same conditions as the other condemned men, in a small cell with a plank bed and one blanket, but no light, was brought to the chapel in handcuffs. The handcuffs were removed for the ceremony and replaced immediately afterwards. He was executed at 3.30 a.m. on Wednesday, 4 May after telling a Capuchin priest, Father Albert, that he was dying for the Glory of God and the Honour of Ireland.

The insurgents had no animus towards the British Tommies. In the last retreat from the GPO George Plunkett risked his life to carry a wounded soldier to safety. Before going out to fight, Pearse told the St Enda's boys always to remember if they won their freedom that it had come through the son of an Englishman. In his last letter to 'My darling Wife, Pulse of my heart', Michael Mallin said that although when thinking of her and their children that his 'heartstrings were torn to pieces' he found:[68] '...no fault with the soldiers or police I forgive them from the Bottom of my heart, pray for all the souls who fell in this fight Irish and English.' For their part individual British officers spoke highly of the rebels. 'They were the cleanest and bravest lot of boys he had ever met' was one officer's verdict. A Captain Shanley, in particular, was recalled as being 'a Christian and a humane man,' and spoken particularly highly of by Connolly, whose last words as the firing party took aim were: 'Father forgive them for they know not what they do'.

In the end it was the English who did not forgive Maxwell. In the aftermath of the Rising, London oscillated between favouring a policy of carrot or stick, without giving Maxwell any clear guidance as to which to pursue. In June he correctly judged that:

Though the Rebellion was condemned it is now being used as a lever to bring on Home Rule, or an Irish Republic. There is a growing feeling that out of Rebellion more has been got than by constitutional methods, hence Mr. Redmond's power is on the wane... It is becoming increasingly difficult to distinguish between a Nationalist and a Sinn Feiner... If there was a General Election, very few if any, of existing Nationalist MPs would be re-elected so there is a danger that Mr Redmond's party would be replaced by others perhaps less amenable to reason. He thought that the major plus of British military policy was that it had taught the rebels that they could never be a match for trained soldiers.

He bore no hostility towards the Irish. On the contrary; Maxwell advocated the installation of an Executive which would 'meet a warm-hearted people half-way in redressing grievances'. Amongst these grievances he cited absentee landlordism and the terrible poverty of Dublin which 'could easily be prevented'. His advice was disregarded and he went the way of the Harrells, the Birrells and the Nathans. By the autumn of 1916 the politicans had made Maxwell a scapegoat for his executions policy, removed him from Ireland and transferred him to the nondescript post of GOC Northern England. He was refused the rank of full General which he had held in Egypt. His most telling judgement was not heeded. In it he concurred with the IRB whose cause his executions policy had done so much to further – the basic cause of the outbreak was the latitude allowed to Carson and the Ulster Volunteers.

Aftermath

After the Rising, events in Ireland proceeded, like bankruptcy, in two ways: gradually and suddenly. Within a few months, public opinion had swung against London so much that the prisoners became more of an embarrassment in jail than at liberty, and by Christmas many were set free, Michael Collins among them. He set about building up both Sinn Fein and the IRB, when he took over the running of the Prisoners' Fund from Kathleen Clarke, Tom Clarke's widow. An actor who played a fleeting role in these pages, Alex McCabe, whom we saw earlier being acquitted for possession of explosives, had a larger part to play in a turning point episode.

One of Collins' initiatives was to put up a prisoner, Joseph McGuinness, as a candidate in a by-election in Longford. The poster showed a man in prison garb with the wording: 'Put him in to get him out'. When the election result was counted, however, it appeared that McGuinness had not got in. The Irish Parliamentary Party candidate had won by a slender margin according to the returning officer. McCabe, who was a very tall man, later described to me what had happened. 'I was wearing the trench coat, the leggings, I must have looked a real IRA man. I jumped up on the platform and I took out my .45 and I stuck it in me man's ear, drew back the hammer and suggested that he might like to think again.' Not unreasonably in the circumstances, the returning officer fell in with this suggestion, and *mirabile dictu*, a box containing 1000 first preference votes for McGuinness was discovered. Sinn Fein was on the march.

They were helped along the route by a combination of infliction and endurance. Thomas Ashe wrote a poem, *Let Me Carry Your Cross for Ireland, Lord*, and became the first hunger striker of the twentieth century to die. Simultaneously, Collins was disproving Maxwell's theory that the rebels had been conclusively taught that they could not successfully contest with trained soldiers. There would be a bloody guerrilla war, an even bloodier civil war, negotiation, partition and the emergence of the two contemporary states of Ireland.

James Craig became the Prime Minister of the smaller state, the six counties, which comprise today's 'Ulster'. This afforded him the opportunity of personally answering the question that he had posed in the House of Commons after the Rising: what steps were being taken to clear out Sinn Fein supporters from the public service? The methods he chose – discriminating and gerrymandering – successfully combated the Catholic birthrate despite sporadic outbreaks of IRA violence, until a civil rights movement arose in the 1960s, chanting not the *Soldiers' Song*, but *We Shall Overcome*. The energies thus released eventually led to a renewal of large-scale hostilities between the Orange and the Green. Both the effects of 1916 on the physical force school of Irish Republicanism and the traditional Tory/Orange relationship could be seen at junctures along the thirty years of violence and bloodshed which followed the Catholic demands for civil rights.

When the Tories took power in June 1970, they immediately replaced Labour's Birrell-like policy with a heavy-handed crackdown on Republicans. Within a few days, a section of the Falls Road in Belfast was placed under curfew and houses ransacked for arms. Provisional IRA recruitment soared and in February 1971, there occurred the first death of a British soldier in the contemporary Troubles. The following August, the Conservatives introduced internment without trial to Northern Ireland. Several hundred Catholics were rounded up, but no Protestants except Ivan Cooper, a civil rights activist and an MP. During the internment period, the British introduced a series of interrogation techniques which eventually led to the Dublin Government charging its British counterpart with torture. The European Court of Human Rights eventually found that the British had been guilty of 'inhuman and degrading treatment'.

One of the very few victims of the interrogation techniques to survive – most died in their forties – was Kevin Hannaway, a cousin of Gerry Adams. When I asked how he had managed to survive a week of hooding, beating, sleep deprivation, hallucinatory drugs and 'white noise', he replied: 'The Last Words; I kept thinking of the last words of the 1916 men, and I said to myself, look at what those men went through. Sure what am I getting – nothin'.'

The Tory/Orange 'Curragh Mutiny' factor was again evident in 1974. A power-sharing Executive between Protestants and Catholics was brought into existence by the Sunningdale Agreement of December 1973, but it was destroyed by what was known as the Loyalist Workers' Strike of 1974. During the strike, which paralysed power plants and sewerage works, barricades were erected across streets by members of the Ulster Defence Association and the UVF. These were manned by masked men armed with clubs, and in some cases, firearms. People could not get to their work and those who did so were openly intimidated. Throughout all this, British Army patrols in full uniform stood idly by alongside the barricades, turning a deaf ear to Nationalists' suggestions that the illegal blockades should cease.

In the twenty years of violence that followed, a more politically minded generation of Republican leadership arose, and eventually entered into behind-the-scenes negotiations which led to the IRA ceasefire of 1994, and ultimately to the Good Friday Agreement. Along the way 1916 sometimes became an uncomfortable memory. How could Pearse and the others be honoured while their inheritors, the Provisional IRA, were condemned? The answer to this question for the Irish Government of the time resulted in a somewhat muted commemoration of the seventy-fifth anniversary of the Rising. For some opponents of Irish Nationalism, the violence led to an effort to downgrade Pearse's reputation in a manner reminiscent of the anti-Casement smear campaign. While admitting that there was no evidence for the theory apart from a line in one of his poems, critics began suggesting that he was homosexual!

Things had changed so much from the time of Hannaway's ordeal that a former top Provisional apologist and activist, the writer Danny Morrison, who has written a play about Pearse, said on RTE[69] as this was being written that when he first went into Long Kesh, the evidence of Pearse's influence was widespread amongst the prisoners in their writings, poetry, design of artefacts and so on. But with equal parts candour and *realpolitique*, Morrison said that at this stage in the Republican struggle, the Provisionals had adopted a 'fundamentalist position'. There was a great difference between those days and the contemporary era, when Sinn Fein was trying 'to manage a Peace Process'.

As Morrison spoke, the wing of Republicanism that does not view Pearse merely as an outdated 'fundamentalist' was gaining recruits by the week. The American State Department[70] reckons that the Real IRA, which bombed Omagh and has made repeated attacks on London, has doubled its size since 1999. As a result, the US has placed the Real IRA on its list of banned terrorist organisations which it is a crime to support.

However, of far more importance than the continuing reputation of an Irish icon, are the equally continuing evidences that the forces which led to 1916 have still not fully died away. In the spring of 2001, during a Westminster election campaign, it became increasingly evident that the progress of the Good Friday Agreement was becoming disturbingly reminiscent of the path of the Home Rule Movement. Firstly, after the ceasefire was declared in August 1994, the Tories in October introduced a new and retarding factor – the decommissioning argument. Although their guns stayed silent, an attempt was made to force the IRA to give up their weapons before they could be admitted to peace talks. Because of this demand, the Peace Process broke down in February of 1996 with the Canary Wharf bombing, but was reinstituted through a combination of American intervention and New Labour's coming to power, independent of the Ulster Unionist MPs at Westminster on whom John Major's administration had depended in its internecine war with the Eurosceptics.

The result of the reinstatement – the Good Friday Agreement – was greeted with a Home Rule-like majority of approval in referenda north and south of the border and widely welcomed in 'the UK mainland'. Yet, at the time of writing, the Agreement is not secure. The fundamentally anti-Catholic, anti-Nationalist wing of Unionism, which joins the Orange Order and votes for Ian Paisley, has made of the Agreement the contemporary variant of the Home Rule issue. Under pressure from this wing the allegedly pro-Agreement segment of Unionism, the Official Unionist Party led by David Trimble, baulked at the idea of sharing power with Sinn Fein and seeks to out-Paisley Paisley in its stentorian demands for decommissioning.

Furthermore, far from meeting the Republican's counterdemands for demilitarisation, the British Army issued a secret directive[71] stating that the Army's objective was to maintain a standing army of at least 10,000 troops in Northern Ireland for the foreseeable future. This was in spite of the fact that at the time the three sovereign governments involved were actively engaged in Peace talks. By way of underlining this viewpoint, the Army built large, expensive forts in the heart of Nationalist areas after the Ceasefire was declared. New Labour has not been any more successful in preventing this situation than was Old Labour during the Workers' Strike of 1974, nor for that matter, the Liberals in the days of Field-Marshal Sir Henry Wilson. The hope of majority opinion on the island of Ireland is that somewhere, somehow, a centre will be found in Unionism that will deliver on the Good Friday Agreement, that the decommissioning problem will be defused and not replaced by some other ploy, that the rise of the Real IRA will be checked, and that the huge majority of people in favour of peace in the island of Ireland will get their way.

This is, in a sense, where we came in – with Unionist opposition to the huge majority in favour of Home Rule, and a small and unrepresentative IRB determined to seize the moment whenever it should arise. True, the Conservative backing for the Unionists is the palest of pale shadows compared with what it was in the days of Milner and Kipling. Nevertheless, as the last days of John Major's government showed, the Conservatives were prepared to play a modern version of the Orange Card in return for Unionist votes at Westminster. It cannot be overlooked that it was the Conservatives who introduced the decommissioning issue into the situation after the Provisional ceasefire was declared. Where the IRB factor is concerned, a spokesperson for the Real IRA explained the movement's policy to me:

> The Unionists will never agree to anything, and when it comes to the crunch, the British won't force them. And in any event, what business do the British have in Ireland anyhow? Force is the only thing they'll listen to.

The Provisional IRA has agreed to legitimise the British presence, recognise the border and place its faith in Sinn Fein's political methods and demographic change. My own belief is that the problem will one day – and perhaps sooner than people believe – be solved by the forces of demography. The results of the census taken on 29 April, 2001 are expected to make it clear that the Nationalist population of the six counties is increasing enormously while that of the

Protestants is ageing and diminishing. Unfortunately for the prospects of enlightened political leadership emerging within the Unionist community and acting in the light of this demographic inevitability, its youth is increasingly obtaining its third level education in the UK whence it does not return. But Ian Paisley's son, who is following in his father's ideological and political footsteps, shows no sign of emigrating, and the British forts still stand provocatively in places like Belfast, Armagh and Tyrone. The Real IRA profits accordingly. So long as these factors obtain, one cannot close the book on 1916. As Yeats wrote after the Rising:

> But who can talk of give and take
> What should be and what not
> While those dead men are loitering there
> To stir the boiling pot.
>
> For those new comrades they have found
> Lord Edward and Wolfe Tone, ...

Since Yeats wrote those words Lord Edward and Wolfe Tone have gained many 'new comrades', including Bobby Sands and the hunger strikers of 1981. To the dismay of Nationalists, the then Secretary of State for Northern Ireland, John Reid, temporarily suspended the Stormont Assembly during August 2001 as a ploy to head off David Trimble's threatened resignation as First Minister of the Northern Assembly over the decommissioning issue. In fact, the correct course would have been to hold new elections. On 14 August, 2001 the IRA responded to this move by withdrawing an offer to cooperate over decommissioning. Nationalists fear that the Unionists are merely using the decommissioning argument in order to avoid sharing power with Catholics, reacting towards the Good Friday Agreement as did their ancestors to the Home Rule Bill almost a century ago. The narrative continues.

Select Bibliography

Readers wishing to pursue the subject of 1916 further will find substantial bibliographies in the scaled-down list which I hereby append. Of my own writings, *The IRA* (HarperCollins), *Michael Collins* and *de Valera* (Hutchinson) deal with 1916 and in the bibliographies and references indicate where further studies may be pursued. Of works written by contemporary figures, I would recommend Piaras Beaslai's *Michael Collins and the Making of a New Ireland* and Dorothy Macardle's *The Irish Republic*, the latter in particular for documents and speeches. Beaslai, being a knowledgeable participant himself, brings unrivalled insights to bear. From the British side, there are the biographies of Sir Henry Wilson by C. E. Callwell (Cassell), and General Sir John Maxwell by Sir George Arthur, which though it does not say much about 1916, does give a valuable insight into the military mindset of the time. Also recommended is *The Revolution in Ireland* by W. Alison Phillips (Longman's). For an insight into how the Dublin Castle system worked, and how the then Chief Secretary Augustine Birrell thought and acted, there are Leon O'Broin's *Dublin Castle and the 1916 Rising* and *The Chief Secretary*, a biography of Birrell. For an informed Unionist perspective, there is Patrick Buckland's *Ulster Unionism* (Gill & Macmillan), and A.T.Q. Stewart's *The Ulster Crisis*. For the actual events of Easter week, there is Edgar Holt's *Protest in Arms* (Putnam), and above all, Max

Caulfield's *Easter Rebellion* (Muller). For this classic work, Caulfield conducted hundreds of interviews with the participants on both sides, as well as drawing on contemporary sources. Both for mentality and the inner machinations of the IRB, there is Sean Cronin's *The McGarrity Papers* (Anvil). And, also for mentality, there is nothing in print to equal Piaras MacLochlainn's *Last Words*, a compendium of the last letters and statements of the executed 1916 leaders, printed by the Kilmainham Jail Restoration Society, Dublin, 1971.

Endnotes

1. *Cathleen Ni Houlihan*, W. B. Yeats, 1902, *The Collected Plays of W. B. Yeats*, Macmillan, New York, 1934.

2. For Churchill's and other Conservative and Unionist policies and speeches see *Ulster Unionism*, Patrick Buckland, Gill & Macmillan, Dublin, 1973.

3. *The Irish Republic*, Dorothy Macardle (4th ed.), Irish Press, Dublin, 1951.

4. Ibid.

5. Quoted in *Wherever Green is Worn*, Tim Pat Coogan, Hutchinson, London, 2000.

6. *The Year of Liberty*, Thomas Pakenham, Literary Guild, London, 1969.

7. Macardle, op.cit.

8. Coogan, op.cit.

9. For a lucid and enlightened account of Irish developments from the Famine to the 1916 period, readers are recommended to *Ireland Since the Famine*, F. S. L. Lyons, Charles Scribner & Sons, New York, 1971.

10. For this and subsequent Conservative and Unionist comments, unless otherwise stated, see Buckland, op.cit.

11. *Edward Carson*, A. T. Q. Stewart, *Gill's Irish Lives* series, published by Gill & Macmillan, Dublin from 1971 onwards.

12. In addition to Buckland, see A.T.Q Stewart's masterly account of the period in *The Ulster Crisis, Resistance to Home Rule, 1912*, Faber & Faber, London, 1967.

13. Quoted in *The IRA*, Tim Pat Coogan, HarperCollins, London, 2000.

14. *Michael Collins and the Making of a New Ireland*, Piaras Beaslai, Vol. 1, Phoenix, Dublin, 1926.

15. Quoted in *Michael Collins*, Tim Pat Coogan, Hutchinson, London, 1990.

16. *Ireland Since the Rising*, Tim Pat Coogan, Pall Mall, London, 1966.

17. Stewart, op.cit., contains the best account of the episode.

18. *The McGarrity Papers*, Sean Cronin, Anvil, Tralee, 1972.

19. Both equally well described in *The Untold Story, the Irish in Canada*, Robert O'Driscoll & Lorna Reynolds ed., Celtic Arts of Canada, Toronto, 1988.

20. Macardle, op.cit.

21. Cronin, op.cit.

22. Macardle, op.cit.

23. Cronin, op.cit.

24. Macardle, op.cit.

25. *Last Words*, Piaras F. MacLochlainn, Kilmainham Jail Restoration Society, Dublin, 2000.

26. *Asgard*, W. Nixon & Capt. Eric Healy, *Coiste an Asgard*, Dublin, 2000.

27. *The Chief Secretary*, Leon O'Broin, Chatto & Windus, London, 1969.

28. See Sean T. O'Kelly, quoted by Macardle, op.cit. and Joseph Lee in *Revising the Rising*, Ni Dhonnachadha and Theo Dorgan, eds., Field Day, Derry, 1991.

29. Interview with author at Irish Hospitals Sweepstakes offices, Dublin, 1965.

30. Macardle, op.cit.

31 Beaslai, op.cit.

32. Quoted in *The Easter Rebellion*, Max Caulfield, Frederick Muller, London, 1963.

33. *Lloyd George, Memoirs of the War*, Vol. 1, Odhams, London, 1938.

34. Birrell to the Royal Commission on Ireland, 1916, quoted by Macardle, op.cit.

35. For Birrell's Irish career, see Leon O'Broin's *The Chief Secretary*, Chatto & Windus, London, 1969 and *Dublin Castle and the 1916 Rising*, Sidgwick & Jackson, London, 1970.

36. Beaslai, op.cit.

37. *Dublin Castle and the 1916 Rising*, Leon O'Broin, Sidgwick & Jackson, London, 1970.

38. 1916 Paper, Box 5608, no.6588, Irish National Archives.

39. For the German contacts with the Irish situation see the works of Cronin, Macardle and Stewart already cited. Also Robert Montieth's *Casement's Last Adventure*, Dublin, 1953 and *The Mystery of the Casement Ship*, Karl Spindler, Berlin, 1931.

40. Both Caulfield and Macardle gave excellent accounts of the final confrontation within the Volunteers on the eve of the Rising.

41. Macardle, op.cit.

42. Cronin, op.cit.

43. Caulfield, op.cit.

44. *Michael Collins*, Tim Pat Coogan, Hutchinson, London, 1990.

45. Ibid.

46. Caulfield, op.cit.

47. The texts of the various Proclamations which appear in this work can be found in either Macardle or Caulfield.

48. *Six Days of the Irish Republic*, William Redmond-Howard, Dublin, 1916.

49. *On Another Man's Wound*, Ernie O'Malley, Anvil Books, Tralee, 1979.

50. Caulfield, op.cit.

51. Coogan, *Michael Collins*, op.cit.

52. Redmond-Howard, op.cit.

53. Caulfield, op.cit.

54. Redmond-Howard, op.cit.

55. Quoted in *Michael Collins*, Tim Pat Coogan.

56. Max Caulfield's account of the last hours in the GPO can hardly be bettered, but readers seeking more information are also recommended to a number of works by survivors of the fighting cited in his bibliography, specifically those by Desmond Ryan and Sean MacLaughlin. Though not a participant, Edgar Holt's *Protest in Arms 1916–23*, Putnam, 1960 is also worth reading.

57. Quoted by MacLochlainn in *Last Words*.

58. MacLochlainn, op.cit.

59. Quoted by Tim Pat Coogan in *de Valera, Long Fellow, Long Shadow*, Hutchinson, London, 1993.

60. Quoted by Macardle, op.cit.

61. Ibid.

62. *Yeats's Poems*, Gill & Macmillan, Dublin, 1989 et seq, Norman Jeffares, ed.

63. WO 141/21 and W141.27, PRO, London.

64. Quoted by MacLochlainn, op.cit.

65. Quoted by Tim Pat Coogan in *Ireland Since the Rising*, Pall Mall, London, 1966.

66. Quoted in MacLochlainn, op.cit.

67. *Grace Gifford Plunkett and Irish Freedom*, Marie O'Neill, Irish Academic Press, Dublin, 2001.

68. Quoted by MacLochlainn, op.cit.

69. The interview took place as part of the major programme on Pearse's life put out by the studio to commemorate the Rising's anniversary in 2001.

70. State Department announcement, 30 April, 2001.

71. GOC Directive to Senior Officers, Northern Ireland, 1997, quoted by Tony Geraghty, *The Irish War*, HarperCollins, 1998.

Index

Abbey Theatre 5, 37
Act of Union [1800] 9, 13
ammunition, explosive 96, 153
arms decommissioning 175, 177
arms importation, ban 44, 53
Asquith, Herbert
    attitude to rebels 145–6
    coalition government 72
    executions 146
    Home Rule 20, 22–3
        attempted reintroduction 150
    visits Dublin 149–50

Bachelors Walk shooting 33, 60
Balfour, Arthur, Home Rule 19
barricades 115, 119
Beaslai, Piaras 32
Belfast
    industries 21–2
    population growth 21
Birrell, Augustine 33–4, 150
    British Army recruitment 74
    Home Rule Bill 20, 73–4
Boland's Bakery 105
Bowen-Colthurst murders 151
Boyne, Battle of the 15
British Army

Bowen-Colthurst murders 151
Directive 78, 176
'inquiries' 153–4
mutinies
    call for 128
    Curragh 42–4
North King Street murders
    151–4
political bias 42, 174
prisoners, treatment of 141–2
recruitment, Ireland 69–72,
    74–5, 77
reinforcements 112–13
tactics 112–13, 119–21, 128–9
taking of GPO 102–3
treatment of Nationalists 73
Ulster, actions in 56, 174, 176
underestimation of 97
British Intelligence, IRB
    German correspondence
        78, 85–6
Brugha, Cathal 117–18
Buckingham Palace Conference
    [1914] 56–7

Canada, IRB invasion 45–6
Carson, Sir Edward

German sympathies 80–1
IRB 28–9, 32
Ulster 27–8, 55
Ulster Covenant 25–7
Casement, Roger 83–4
   execution 91, 144
   gun running 90–1
   visits Germany 84–5
Castlelyons 110
casualties
   civilians 103, 107–8
   total 142
Cathleen Ni Houlihan [play]
   5–6
Catholic Defenders 14
Catholic emancipation 16
ceasefire, Pearse orders 138
'Celtic Dawn' 38–9
Childers, Robert Erskine, gun
   running 58–9
Churchill, Lord Randolph 6–8,
   16
civilians
   Bowen-Colthurst murders 151
   casualties 103, 107–8, 142
   humanity towards 114–15
   North King Street murders
      151–6
   reaction to prisoners 141, 142
   shooting of 151–2, 153–4
Clan na Gael 47, 50
Clanwilliam House 105, 114–15,
   120, 122–3
Clarke, Kathleen 160–3
Clarke, Thomas James 48–50
   execution 143, 160–3
   IRB Military Council 66
   Irish Volunteers 52–3
Colbert, Con 144
College of Surgeons 106
Collins, Michael 98–9, 125–7
   German gun running 87–8
   release from prison 171
Connolly, James 39–40, 41, 126
   execution 144, 159–60
   injuries 130–1
   IRB Military Council 66
   Irish Citizen Army 39–40
   statement of position 132–5
   surrender order 140
Connolly, Nora 95, 158–60
Connolly, Rory 97, 158
Conservative and Unionist
   Party
   German war decision 80
   Home Rule Bill 22–3
   'Orange Card' 8, 16, 22–3, 177
   Republican crackdown 172–3
   Unionist cooperation 6–8, 177
Cosgrave, William 117–18
court martials
   Bowen-Colthurst 151
   in camera 143, 151, 156–7
   publication 156–8

Crown Alley Telephone
    Exchange 106
Curragh Mutiny 42–4

Daly, Edward 144
de Valera, Eamon 51–2
    execution commuted 145
    leadership 123–5
    Mount Street defence 115–16
    surrender 141
Defence of the Realm Act [1914]
    75–6, 79
demography
    Ireland 38
    Ulster 177–8
Devoy, John 47, 82–3
Directive 78, 176
Dublin
    loyalism in 33
    poverty 39
Dublin Castle, attack on 105
Dublin Fusiliers 128
Dublin lockout [1913] 39
Dungannon Clubs 47–8

Emmet, Robert 15–16, 68
executions
    intention to carry out 157
    limitations on 145
    memorial cards 158
    rebel leaders 143–4
Executive [Ireland] 33, 35–6, 86

famines, Ireland 13, 16, 17
Fianna Eireann 40–1, 50
Fingal, Rising in 110
Four Courts 105, 116, 137
France
    Catholic alliances 11
    immigration from 21

Gaelic Athletic Association
    37–8, 50
Gaelic League 37–8, 50
General Post Office
    advance on 98
    military reaction 102
    republican flags 100, 141
    shelling of 125–6, 137
    taking of 98–9, 100, 102–3
Georgius Rex veterans 111–12
Germany
    Casement's visits 84–5
    Irish Brigade 84–5
    Nationalist sympathies 68, 78,
        80, 83, 86–90
    Unionist sympathies 80–2
Gladstone, William Ewart 17
Good Friday Agreement
    [1998], Home Rule parallel
    2, 175–6
Grace, James 72, 113–14
Grangegorman Lunatic Asylum
    102
Grattan, Henry 10

Griffith, Arthur 37
gun running
    German 80, 86–90
    Irish Volunteers 59–60
    UVF 44, 54

Heuston, Sean 144
Hobson, Bulmer 91
Home Rule Bills
    1886 7–8, 16
    1912 20, 22–3, 61
        coalition government 72–3
        reintroduction 150
        Suspensory Act 61
Howth gun running 59–60, 96, 153
human rights abuses, British 173
Hyde, Douglas 37–8

independence proclamation 127–8
industrialisation, rise of 21–2
internment without trial 173
interrogation 143, 173
IRA [Irish Republican Army] 174, 176–7
Irish Brigade 84–5
Irish Citizen Army 39–40, 41
Irish Coercion Act [1887] 19
Irish Freedom [newspaper] 50
Irish Home Rule League 16

Irish identity 36–7, 38
Irish Parliamentary Party
    appeal on executions 146
    hostility to 48
    Parnell 18–20
    Redmond 20
Irish Republican Brotherhood [IRB]
    aims 31–2
    Canada, invasion of 45–6
    formation 44–5
    Germany
        assistance from 68, 78, 86–7
        links with 78, 85–6
    Home Rule support 18–20
    infiltration by 50
    Military Council 65–6
    Rising 62, 68, 86
Irish Volunteers
    formation 51–4
    IRB split 68–9
    Mansion House meeting 70–1
    National Volunteers split from 71–2
    proposed 51
    Redmond's control of 60
    Rising 93–6
    UVF 51

Jacob's Biscuit Factory 105
Jameson's Distillery 105
Joyce, James 99–100

Kent, Eamonn 66, 117, 144
Kent, Thomas 144
Kipling, Rudyard 30
Kitchener, Lord Horatio 73

Labour Party, policy on Ireland
    176
Land League 17
land reform 21
Law, Andrew Bonar 23–5, 56
Liberal Unionists 8
Liberty Hall 78
Linenhall Barracks, capture of
    133, 135
looting 103–4
Louth [County], Rising in 111
Lowe, Brig. Gen. W.H.M.
    102–3, 121
  acceptance of surrender 139
  King Street killings 154
Loyalist Workers' Strike 173–4

MacBride, Maj. John 144
MacDermott, Sean 66, 144
MacDonagh, Thomas 66, 67
  execution 144
  IRB Military Council 66
McGuinness, Joseph 171–2
MacNeill, Eoin 50–1
  Irish Volunteers 69, 91–2
  opposition to violence 79
Maconchy, Col. 123

Mallin, Michael 144
Malone, Capt. Michael 113–14,
    122
Markham, Thomas 35–6
Markievicz, Lady Constance
    40–1
  College of Surgeons strong-
    point 106
  Fianna Eireann 50
  Irish Citizen Army 40, 41
  St Stephen's Green fighting
    115
Maxwell, Gen. Sir John Grenfell
    135–6, 143, 168–9
Milner, Lord Alfred 42–3
Moore Street 137
Mount Street 111–12, 118

Nathan, Sir Matthew 33, 78
National Volunteers 72
Nelson's Pillar 100, 129
North King Street murders
    151–6
Northumberland Road 105, 114,
    119–22

O'Connell, Daniel 16
O'Farrell, Elizabeth, surrender
    negotiations 138–9, 140
O'Hanrahan, Michael 144
O'Kelly, Sean T. 62
O'Mahony, John 45–6

O'Rahilly, The 92–3, 97–8
Orange Order 6–9, 14, 15

Parnell, Charles Stewart 18–20
partition 3, 57
Peace Process 2, 175–6
Pearse, Padraig 62–5, 66, 126,
    131–2, 163
  court martial 164
  execution 143, 165
  Independence proclamation
    127–8
  IRB Military Council 66
  mobilisation 91–2
  Morrison play 174
  Provisional Government
    proclamation 100
  smear campaign 174
  surrender 137–40
Phoenix Park barracks 107
Plunkett, Joseph Mary 67–8, 98
  execution 144, 166–7
  IRB Military Council 66
  marriage in prison 166–7
  Rising 68, 108–9
  visits Germany 85
Portal, Col. 129, 138
Presbyterians 9–10, 12
prisoners
  British ill-treatment of 141–2
  executions 143–4
  innocent 150

  interrogation 143, 173
  release 171
  Republican treatment of 116
proclamations
  independence 127–8
  Maxwell 136
  Provisional Government 100,
    101
  Wimborne 106–7
Protestant Volunteers [1782]
  9–10
Provisional IRA 2, 173
Provisional [Revolutionary]
  Government 66
  Peace Conference 137
  proclamation 100, 101

Real IRA 175, 176–7
rebellions
  1798 11–12
  1867 46
recruitment, British Army
  69–72, 74–5, 77
Redmond, John 20, 60, 69, 70–1
rent boycotts 17
Rossa, O'Donovan 63–4
Royal Commission of Enquiry
  150
Royal Irish Constabulary 35–6

Sackville Street, damage 131–2
Scottish settlers ('planters')

14–15, 22
Shaw, George Bernard 146–7
Sinn Fein
  discrimination against 172
  divisions 48
  foundation 37
  Parliamentary representation
    171–2
South Dublin Union [*later* St
  James's Hospital] 105,
  116–17
South Staffordshire Battalion
  152–4
St Enda's school for boys 63
St Stephen's Green 105, 115
Stephens, James 44–5
Sunningdale Agreement [1973]
  173
surrender
  accepted 137–41
  negotiated 137–40
Suspensory Act [1914], Home
  Rule Bill 61

Tone, Theobald Wolfe 11–12

Ulster

demographic changes 177–8
German support for 80–2
political definition 31, 57
Province 31
Ulster Covenant [1912] 25–7,
  42–3
Ulster Unionist Council 28
Ulster Volunteer Force [UVF]
  arms smuggling 44
  formation 27
  illegal activities 27
  Irish Volunteers 51
  proposed coup 57
  war service 61
United Irishmen 11–12
USA
  attitude to executions 145
  IRB in 45–7
  Irish immigration 13, 17

White, Capt. Jack 41
Wimborne, Ivor, Baron 78,
  106–7, 150

Yeats, W.B. 5, 36–7, 149
Young Irelanders 16